The Lost Arts *of* Hearth and Home

The Lost Arts *of* Hearth and Home

The Happy Luddite's Guide to Self-Sufficiency

A RECONDITE TREASURY OF ARCANE SECRETS, WHEREIN ARE EXPLAINED MYSTERIES OF THE KITCHEN AND CUPBOARD, PLAINLY SET FORTH FOR THOSE WHO WOULD PROFIT MATERIALLY AND SPIRITUALLY THROUGH SELF-SUFFICIENCY, HONEST UNPLUGGED LABOR, AND DILIGENT APPLICATION OF ECONOMIC PRINCIPLES DERIVED FROM OUR ESTEEMED FOREBEARS IN MATTERS BOTH ESCULENT AND DOMESTIC.

KEN ALBALA and
ROSANNA NAFZIGER HENDERSON

A PERIGEE BOOK

A PERIGEE BOOK
Published by the Penguin Group
Penguin Group (USA) Inc.
375 Hudson Street, New York, New York 10014, USA

Penguin Group (Canada), 90 Eglinton Avenue East, Suite 700, Toronto, Ontario M4P 2Y3, Canada (a division of Pearson Penguin Canada Inc.) • Penguin Books Ltd., 80 Strand, London WC2R 0RL, England • Penguin Group Ireland, 25 St. Stephen's Green, Dublin 2, Ireland (a division of Penguin Books Ltd.) • Penguin Group (Australia), 250 Camberwell Road, Camberwell, Victoria 3124, Australia (a division of Pearson Australia Group Pty. Ltd.) • Penguin Books India Pvt. Ltd., 11 Community Centre, Panchsheel Park, New Delhi—110 017, India • Penguin Group (NZ), 67 Apollo Drive, Rosedale, Auckland 0632, New Zealand (a division of Pearson New Zealand Ltd.) • Penguin Books (South Africa) (Pty.) Ltd., 24 Sturdee Avenue, Rosebank, Johannesburg 2196, South Africa
Penguin Books Ltd., Registered Offices: 80 Strand, London WC2R 0RL, England

THE LOST ARTS OF HEARTH AND HOME

Illustrations by Marjorie Nafziger

First edition: October 2012

ISBN: 978-0-399-53777-6

An application to catalog this book has been submitted to the Library of Congress.

PRINTED IN THE UNITED STATES OF AMERICA

To Mildred Q. Pilchard,
font of all wisdom and virtue,
our undying gratitude

CONTENTS

4. *Fish* 79

5. *Dairy and Eggs* 89

6. *Desserts* 111

7. *Brewing and Distillation* 127

8. *Nostrums and Household Stuffe* 141

9. *Sewing* 165

To the Gentle Reader,

We are so happy to see you again, dear friends. In this, our sequel to the *Lost Art of Real Cooking*, we venture beyond the kitchen, scurrying down sundry corridors, to spread the spirit of antiquated self-sufficiency throughout the household. Well, to be honest, we had such fun and became so accustomed to testing recipes for the first book, that we never stopped. Then it occurred to us that most cookbooks in the past also included medicinal recipes, perfumes, hints about household maintenance, and sometimes décor tips. Why not include all these, too?

Our goal is not, it should be pointed out, homesteading. We don't keep animals, plant crops, weave our own clothes, or live in a sod house on the prairie. Though that sounds like a lot of fun, we are both city dwellers with day jobs, Rosanna in San Francisco and Ken 90 miles inland in Stockfish, California. We expect our readers will be much like us: people who love to cook, love fresh natural ingredients and old techniques for preservation; people who like doing things themselves with a needle and thread, garden hoe or handsaw. Most important, we are writing for people who are fed up with the way modern food industries (and other household industries) connive to get us to buy things under the pretext that they will make life quicker, easier, and more convenient. We like doing things the slower way—so that first and foremost food tastes good and the objects we live with are aesthetically pleasing and useful. Our tastes are decidedly old-fashioned, not to the point of rejecting everything modern, but saving those precious things most people never think of doing themselves anymore.

In this book we have also decided to go a little more unplugged, flirt with techniques a little more daring and dangerous, and trust old cookbooks and our instincts a little more than before. Thus you will find more open fires than electric ovens here, more jars on shelves than in the fridge—in fact we like to think of our approach to preservation as pre-Pasteurian. There are also more ambitious projects, things that, quite frankly, frightened us at first. They have since become second nature. We also invested in some more antiquated equipment, like a stone quern for grinding grain and a copper still for making electuaries. Neither was very expensive and we will offer alternatives for those enthusiasts not quite as committed as ourselves—yet.

We also realized while writing this that there is no point in offering you recipes for really complex technical procedures when expert books are readily available on topics like brewing and cheese making. Our intention is merely to get you started, as amateurs like us. We would like to help you think about things you would never have thought possible without a professional manual, thousand of dollars of equipment, and a degree in biochemistry. People in the past had none of these and neither do we. Yet as you will see, some of the things we have accomplished through pure gumption, perseverance, and a lot of sweat are perfectly feasible within a modest budget.

We should also point out that this book is written in a particularly old-fashioned style without precise measurements, cooking times, or unnecessary minutiae that would otherwise prevent you from unleashing your creative energy in the kitchen and workshop. We sincerely dislike the modern recipe format and hope you will come to appreciate how liberating it can be to just wing it, as we like to say. The recipes do really work; you just need to trust yourselves.

The Lost Arts *of* Hearth and Home

1

Grains

Lately we've noticed some fabulous ancient grains popping up in the market. Not that we could ever abandon our favorite wheat, but in this chapter we give you some fresh ideas for cooking grains, using the oldest techniques we could muster. As you will see, the extra effort of processing them yourself will pay off in exquisite flavor, and quite possibly health as well, so whenever possible we suggest starting with whole grains.

You can buy excellent bread flour anywhere nowadays. Although grinding it yourself is more difficult, it is infinitely more satisfying. You don't need a high-tech flour mill, only the most primitive technology, hailing back ten millennia: the stone quern. You can still buy one. It's a simple mechanism consisting of one large concave stone with a handle on top. It has notches cut into the interior that fit over a fixed bottom stone, which is convex with notches. Grain is poured into a hole in the top, and as the top stone is rotated by hand, the grain is crushed and sprinkles out the sides where the two stones meet. Bigger versions with millstones weighing several tons that were turned by oxen or by huge waterwheels work basically the same way. Modern milling differs by using steel rollers. If you don't have a quern, you can find other simple grain mills for sale, or better yet, try a huge vertical hollow log and a pounding stick.

It takes a lot of work to mill flour this way, but it's fun and good exercise. It will take maybe half an hour, milling handful by handful, to get three cups of flour, or enough for a standard loaf of bread. It also helps if you pass the flour through a fine sieve; you'll see a lot of coarser bits are left behind. Cook these up as you would cream of wheat, or just throw them back into the mill and grind again. The flour can be used as you would any flour, but keep in mind that since it's *whole* whole wheat, it will

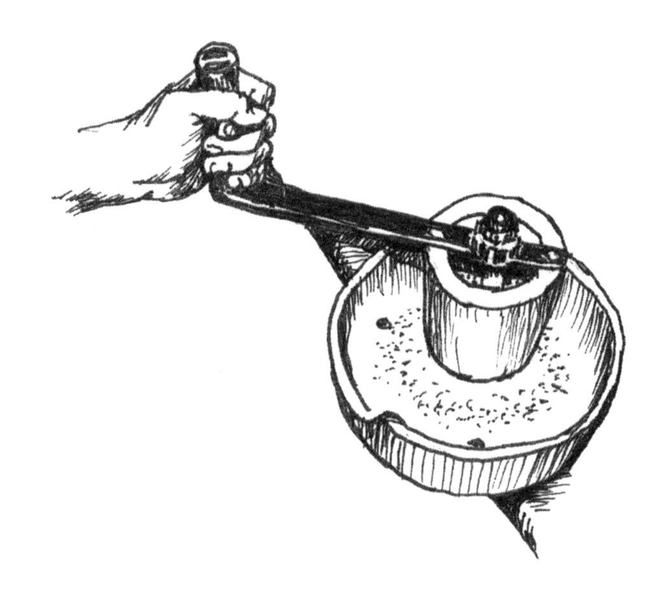

absorb a lot of water, but slowly, and it will take longer to rise if you're making bread because it has a dense texture. It definitely does work though, and yields a really complex, fresh-tasting earthy crumb, quite unlike other flours.

Wheat is grown right near where I live in Stockton, California. It was the first major crop in this area, the wheat being sent up to the gold mines after 1848. Back then, the water wasn't diverted by canals and levies, so the land was irrigated by natural flooding, which is why the Caterpillar tractor was invented in these parts. Ben Holt figured out that switching wheels for a rotating metal tread would prevent the tractor from sinking into the muddy soil. There were also huge mills in town, the Sperry Flour Mill building on the canal downtown is just the last of them. Eating local wheat feels like a taste of history, but finding such wheat for sale is very difficult for some of us, and the flour in our local stores is shipped from the other side of the country. Do you know how hard it is to buy plain local wheat? It's not in the phone book. Call one agricultural agency and they will pass you on to another. A third will charge you $200 for this information. Another says they can give you names but not phone numbers. In the end the nice people at the California Wheat Commission Board said they would send me a sample, especially because it was for educational purposes. It cost $5 just to ship across town. Nonetheless, the wheat was very fresh and delicious.

If you really want to get a sense of the immense labor involved, try growing your own wheat. I happened to be touring an experimental farm in Finland with a group of ethnologists and pocketed a handful of plucked grains, which no one seemed to mind. You, however, can buy whole wheat berries or try a mix of wheat, rye, barley, and oats. Just make sure the berries aren't hybridized, in which case they won't bear grains. If you live in a cold climate, start germination once danger of frost is past with spring wheat; in warm places, start in the fall with winter wheat. Sprout the grains in the house in a self-sealing plastic bag with a little water. Place the bag on the windowsill; once the berries have little rootlets, plant them in the ground or even in a big clay pot. They will grow tall and begin to look dry, at which point cut them and get a stick or make a flail to beat out the grains (that's two sticks connected with a chain—the thing that pharaohs hold along with the shepherd's crook). Then winnow them in a basket by tossing the contents up in the air; the chaff blows away with the wind. For my handful of planted grain I got just a little over a handful of grain! If you have some space to plant sprouted wheat in the ground with good sun, your yield ratio should be much better than mine. I used the flour made from my harvest for a fresh new bread starter, which turned out ferociously strong.

Absolutely Antiquated Bread

To get started on making bread, begin with a starter. Add 1 cup of flour and 1 cup of untreated, nonchlorinated, spring water to a large bowl and mix well. Add a little more flour and water every day for about 2 weeks. Smells nice and sour? That's your levain. There is no reason to add commercial yeast to this. Yeast is everywhere, and it's free. Add about 2 cups of this to 1 cup of water and enough flour to make a moist dough. Add about 1 tablespoon of sea salt. Knead thoroughly for about 15 minutes.

Cover in a bowl and let sit about 2 hours, then knock down and form either into a round ball or, if you like, put it in a lightly greased flowerpot-shaped unglazed earthenware vessel. This is how the ancient Egyptians made bread, and the form makes baking a breeze, because you just put the whole thing in the oven. The dough will take anywhere from 8 to 14 hours to rise. Overnight is ideal. When ready to bake, stoke your wood-fired oven for about 1 hour until blazing hot (directions are on page 244) or crank up your conventional oven to 550°F and splash some water inside to create steam. If you're baking the bread free form, slash the bread several times on top and transfer to the oven with a peel, sliding carefully onto a baking stone. Bake until brown and crusty. Let cool. If you have used the pot to bake, let it cool thoroughly before you turn the bread out. Devour like a hungry slave. Then build some pyramids.

—K

Effortless Sourdough Bread with Whey or Brine

Just a bit of whey or brine and a long fermentation produce a savory, sour bread when you don't have immediate access to a sourdough starter. This recipe starts out as a false sourdough (yeasted, rather than made with a starter), but eventually becomes a true one. The loaves are heavy but full of chewy holes and intensely flavorful. I call it *effortless* because you don't have to maintain the starter; just save a bit of dough in the fridge for your next batch. This bread makes excellent use of coarsely ground rye or spelt, which means you can avoid the extra trouble of getting the flour nice and fine if you're grinding it yourself. Of the home-ground slow-rising breads, this has become my quick and sloppy standby. It takes about 24 hours from start to finish and is indeed sloppy enough that it requires loaf pans.

My grain mill holds 1½ pounds of whole rye or wheat berries in its hopper, which conveniently makes one loaf of bread. I told you it was heavy bread. This grain can be very coarsely ground. Some of the grains should be just cracked, rather than ground, but there should be some finer flour in the mix, too. You could approximate this effect with store-bought flour by including some cracked wheat—in any case, use 1½ pounds per loaf.

Put the flour in a large bowl and add 1 tablespoon of salt per loaf. The first time you make this bread, dissolve a tiny pinch of dry yeast in ¼ cup of lukewarm water. No more than ⅛ teaspoon yeast per loaf.

You can use whey (not salted) for some or all of the liquid in this recipe, or you can use a little pickle brine and water for the rest of the liquid. Don't use more than ¼ cup of pickle brine per loaf; if it's very salty, use less or no salt in the flour. Add the yeast mixture and 1 or 2 cups of the chosen liquid per loaf. Stir well. Continue adding liquid until the dough reaches a thick porridge-like consistency. The coarse grains will slowly absorb the liquid, but even once they do, the dough should be too soft to knead by hand.

Stir it vigorously with a large sturdy spoon for 5 to 10 minutes, until it looks thicker and more ropey. Cover the bowl with a tea towel or plate, making sure there is plenty of room for the dough to rise. Dough this wet will stick terribly to your towel.

Let it rise for about 8 hours at cool room temperature—overnight is fine. Stir it down and let it rise for another 8 hours. Stir the dough down again and scoop out ½ cup or so of dough. Put it in a covered jar and store it in the refrigerator.

I use 5- by 8½-inch loaf pans for this bread. I wouldn't use anything smaller, but other shapes and sizes will work so long as the loaf gets adequate support.

Grease your loaf pans well and scoop or pour the dough into the pan. Wet your hand thoroughly and use your palm to smooth the surface of the dough. Whereas you would usually knead your dough to create a taut gluten film on the surface, here the dough is so wet you create a smooth gluten film by caressing it with your hand.

Let the dough rise, again at cool room temperature, until it's level with the tops of the pans, or a little bit higher. This rising is more of a softening and bubbling—a 15 percent increase, not a big inflation. You want to particularly avoid letting the bread overrise, or it will spill out of the pans when baking and have a loose, crumbly texture. The rising may take 1 to 3 hours or more, depending on room temperature and the mood of the yeast.

Preheat the oven to 425°F and pop the loaves in. Let them bake for 30 minutes, then reduce the temperature to 375°F and let them bake another 20 to 30 minutes. They're done when the bread has pulled away slightly from the edges and is well browned. Let them cool for 15 minutes in the pans, then turn them out on a board to finish cooling. You really must resist cutting into this bread before it's all the way cool or it might collapse.

The saved dough will stay alive in the fridge for several months between bakings, although using it every few weeks is better. From now on when you bake this bread, don't use any dry yeast. Instead, add the saved dough when you're mixing it up. You also don't have to use whey or brine, as the lactic acid bacteria are already established in the old dough, but you can add some if you have extra that needs to be used up.

—R

Couscous

Don't get me wrong, on those occasions when we are rushed there is nothing better than instant couscous. A little chicken stock brought to a boil, maybe a few saffron threads if we're feeling indulgent. In goes the couscous; 10 minutes tops, but it isn't really couscous. If you want to have fun making couscous, try doing it from scratch. You won't match the Berber woman whose dexterous hands have perfected the process in the course of a lifetime, but your couscous will still be very good. Begin with about 1 cup of semolina flour, the coarse yellow kind, and 1 cup of bread flour. Put the flours on a large platter and just sprinkle water over. Rub your palms in a circular motion over it, picking some up every now and then and rubbing it between your palms. What you are trying to do is separately coat every single tiny speck of semolina with the bread flour. It should be on the dry side, so add more flour if necessary. Let it dry thoroughly on the platter. Then wrap the couscous in a dishcloth and tie the top with string. Put it in a steamer, or better yet a proper couscousier, set over a pot of simmering spicy meat stew. It's basically just a steaming chamber set on top of a regular pot. The gentle aromatic steam of whatever you're cooking below cooks and flavors the semolina granules. When done, fluff the couscous with a fork and serve on the platter with the stewed meat. For full gastronomic effect, use three fingers of the right hand to eat, just as they do in northern Africa.

—K

Croissants

My father was a rather picky eater, but he loved pastry more than most things on earth. I remember driving for hours to buy a big box of sticky buns in the Pennsylvania Dutch Country or waking up early Sunday morning and driving into Freehold, New Jersey, to be the first in line at Freedman's Bakery for coffee cakes, pound cake, Danish, babka, and pastries of every shape and size. His most impressive trick was immediately upon pulling into a new town, he would hop out of the car and put his nose in the air, sniffing in every direction. Despite never having never set foot in the place, my father could navigate, by smell alone, to the nearest bakery. I saw this many times. Even more intriguing, he would buy one of practically everything behind the counter and systematically break open each one. He'd judge each—"Nope, garbage." "Too greasy."—until finally landing on something that satisfied his discerning palate.

Strangely, pastries and cakes are among those things I never cared for much. But there is one irresistible pastry that's so simple, I can't imagine why most cookbooks make such an ordeal out of it. Think of the perfect light crispy buttery croissant, with layers that invite manual dissection, leaving shards of flaky dough all over the place. The croissants at the store are just disgusting, soft and laden with shortening. So here's how to do it yourself.

Make a simple yeast dough: 1 packet of yeast and 3 cups of flour, but instead of water use 1 cup of milk, 1 tablespoon of melted and cooled butter, and a good pinch of salt. Let it rest a while and roll it out flat. Then take two sticks of very cold butter and roll them out between two sheets of plastic wrap until the same size as the dough and as thin as you can get it. It need not be exact, measured, or precise in any dimension. Sorry, Martha. Pull away one layer of plastic wrap and lay the butter sheet over the dough. Then pull away the top sheet of plastic wrap and fold the dough over twice. Throw it in the fridge. Wait a while, roll it out, and then fold it over again. And again. And a fourth time won't hurt. Make that five. The idea is to get many, many thin layers of butter in between the layers of dough. Finally roll it out one last time and cut into long triangles. Cut a notch at the base, so they'll curve nicely at the end. Then roll the triangles up starting at the wide base and curve them around into crescents. Let them rise at room temperature until puffy. Brush with egg wash and bake for 30 to 35 minutes at 400°F. Easy peasy.

Now here's the really fun part. Inside these you can put whatever you like. Grate some good dark chocolate or spread on cinnamon, sugar, and walnuts. Even jam works fine. If you are feeling really adventurous, throw in ham and cheese or bacon. Anything tastes good baked in a croissant.

—K

Dumplings

Before Prague became a popular tourist spot and good restaurants began to proliferate, there were still some Soviet-era eateries that served solid nourishing stodge for stalwart comrades. These eateries were not simply decorated, mind you. There were flashing lights, mirrors, loud Eurotrash music, and garish decor. If that bothered you, you had to find one of the quiet floors, often underground, where they sent the old folks. Dvořák or Smetana would be playing. Here was Party-approved *traditional* Czech fare, mostly meat and potatoes and gravy, but made honestly. Unless you have been walking all day in the cold, I would not recommend it. But under such circumstances, a simple dumpling can be a thing of consummate beauty and grace. Not light and fluffy, but leaden, dripping with fat, sodden with gravy, chewy, and potentially deadly if lobbed at your dining partner, who turns out to be an undercover spy. I was served three different dumplings one cold day, one made of rye bread chunks, another of sourdough, and the third of fine crumbs laden with paprika and lard.

Here's the rule: Never ever throw away stale bread. In fact, leave some bread out just for breadcrumbs or dumplings. I keep a good quarry in a big mortar and use either a grater for a small amount or pound it up into fine crumbs for larger projects. The most interesting dumplings are made from just coarsely bashed-up stale bread and egg. For rye dumplings, I suggest adding in a few handfuls of crumbs, some dill, mustard powder, salt and pepper, and an egg. Have a pot of your best stock boiling. Moisten the mix with a little stock and let it sit, just until you can roll it into balls. You should add a little flour, too, for extra insurance, so they don't fly apart in the pot. Once you've rolled out balls, whatever size you want, drop them into the gently simmering stockpot. You can let them cook just until they float up and then serve as soup, or even better, leave them there to simmer an hour or so. These are not served like matzoh balls in soup, though you surely can do so, but as a side dish. Put them next to some pot roast or a good hunk of braised pork. Dump on the gravy and go to town.

Now for the variations: You can use any kind of bread and embellish the dumplings with any number of flavorings. A dose of chicken fat and paprika is lovely, as is crumbled bacon with a few drizzles of the drippings. In Italy, traditionally, such early forms of gnocchi were made with stale breadcrumbs, flour, and grated cheese. Serve just with some melted butter. You can also mix in ricotta with fine breadcrumbs and egg; these are very delicate. You are also only a few steps away from a French quenelle. Let's say you have no breadcrumbs: Then feel free to use leftover potatoes mashed up with egg and flour rolled into little balls. Leftover rice works well, too. Imagine you have some exotic kind of flour around, like buckwheat or chestnut. These make some of the most interesting dumplings imaginable. Just add some egg, milk, and seasonings; roll into balls; and toss in the pot.

The dumpling is among those few truly easy, economical, and eminently adaptable foods that for reasons that confound me have gone utterly out of fashion. Try it, especially in the winter, and you may eschew mashed potatoes and pasta for a while.

—K

Panisses

Related to dumplings are a whole slew of tasty dishes made of pulmentum—or porridge, spread in a baking pan, cut up, and then fried. The original ancient Roman version was made with barley, and of course, corn has taken its place today as polenta. But equally ancient is millet. You probably know it as birdseed. It has an intriguing mucilaginous quality that holds it together. Just cook it in a roughly equal part milk with some butter and salt until thick, pour it out onto a greased baking sheet, and let it cool. Cut into squares or little finger shapes, then fry in a skillet in butter or oil. They put French fries to shame. The exact same thing can be done with chickpea flour, which you can buy in a health food store, an Italian grocery, or even an Indian grocery, where it's called besan. In France they call these crispy little fingers *panisses*. If you go into a health food store you can also find some amazingly tasty ancient grains like quinoa and amaranth. Even chia has been showing up lately—the same stuff sprouted Chia Pets are made from, a tiny black seed. All these make fabulous porridge and even better panisses, cooked exactly the same way. Incidentally, you can also deep fry these if you like them super crunchy.

—K

Dosas

Huge Indian crepes, called *dosas*, are pretty tricky to prepare. You need a really large flat cooking surface; a flattop griddle is ideal. A big skillet works all right, as does a paella pan. Take

1 cup (or more) of urad dahl—these are little black beans in the mung family, but once the outer coating is removed, they're white and look sort of like lentils or split peas. Soak the urad dahl in plenty of water overnight. Do the same with twice the amount of rice, good fragrant basmati in this case. Drain the grains and put them together in a big mortar and grind into a fine paste. If you must use a machine to grind, go ahead. Add water to this to make a smooth batter, and leave it out for a day until it starts to bubble and smells a little sour.

When you're ready to cook the dosas, get your pan to medium heat and put in a little ghee or clarified butter. The odd trick here is to sprinkle a little water onto the cooking surface after you've added the butter and wipe it off with a paper towel or cloth, so you really have only the barest residue of butter to prevent the dosas from sticking. Pour in a ladleful of batter and quickly swirl it around with the bottom of the ladle until it covers the entire surface. You may need to thin the batter out and you may find that swirling the pan itself is easier. However you do it, these should be paper thin and crisp on the edges. Turn over deftly with a spatula and cook for another 30 seconds or so. You will also want to cool the pan a little between each dosa, again with a sprinkle of water, or the batter will cook too quickly before it spreads. You can just serve dosas as is, maybe with a smudge of yogurt and some diced cucumber or some chutney, or fill them with an elaborate curry. Or best, serve with a nice sour tamarind-spiked sambar, which is basically a spicy vegetable stew with pigeon peas.

This exact same batter can also be steamed to make idli, which are puffy little cakes. In southern India you can find special steamers with inset molds to make delicate disks of dough. You can easily put little shallow condiment bowls or ramekins into a bamboo steamer for a comparable effect. But if you want to try a wild technique, loosely stretch a fine linen dishcloth over the top of a pot of simmering water and secure with a rubber band or string. Then pour some of the batter directly onto the cloth and put a lid on. Make sure not to stretch the cloth too tight or you won't get a nicely mounded idli.

—K

Crepes

Crepes are charming, sophisticated yet earthy, downright lovable in every way, without being dowdy like their cousin the pancake. I once made several hundred that were rolled into blintzes for a Jewish food festival. Six pans going at once on burners; someone else rotating the pans as I poured and swirled batter. Now that was serious fun. The recipe I usually use is very simple. The batter is made from 1½ cups of flour—preferably pastry flour with a low gluten content—2 eggs, vanilla, 1 teaspoon of baking powder, 1 or 2 spoons of sugar, and enough whole milk to make a light, very thin batter. Also add in a few tablespoons of melted butter for unctuousness. Let the batter sit a while. Fry these up in butter in a *very* hot nonstick pan, as thin as you can. Swirling the pan is the trick for even distribution. No need to turn them over. Just remove from the pan and stack them up as you go. Fill the cooled crepes with a mixture of cream cheese, cottage cheese, sugar, and vanilla. Fold over the lower end, then the two sides, and roll them up neatly. A dab of raspberry jam on top is lovely. Or you can put anything savory in your crepes, such as a slice of ham and cheese. The French put practically anything inside.

Crepes really start becoming interesting when you use different kinds of flour. The classic in Brittany is the buckwheat crepe. Unlike any other grain, you can actually buy whole buckwheat groats and crush them in a mortar or whizz them in a blender easily. They're actually not a grain but a fruit, from a plant in the rhubarb and sorrel family. Buckwheat has a nutty deep flavor that is incomparable and works with the basic crepe recipe above. Chestnut flour is also excellent. The Italians use it in some very interesting desserts like castagnaccio, a kind of dense cake studded with raisins and pine nuts and sometimes rosemary or fennel. But you can also make chestnut flour crepes; the only difference between these and the thick castagnaccio is the addition of eggs and some butter and pouring the thinned batter into a pan, rather than baking as a cake. With a fruity jam, like apricot or raspberry, these are heavenly.

In this same family are the legion of dishes variously called farinata or socca, made from chickpea flour. All these flours can be bought at an Italian grocery or online. The farinata is a kind of cake made with olive oil, baked in a super-hot oven so it's crunchy on top and soft in the middle. But a thin pliable crepe version is perfectly viable, and again the basic recipe just given works fine, though there's no reason to include sugar because chickpeas have a natural sweetness. I've eaten magnificent ones from a cart in Nice, plain and succulent.

—K

Acorn Crepes

Of all these sundry variations, the most interesting and ancient, and the most difficult to process, are acorn crepes. The technical term, and one of my favorite words, is *balanophagy*, from the Greek *balanos* (acorn) and *phagein* (to eat). Let us do as the Native Americans of California did for centuries and centuries, to process what was their essential staple. Start by collecting acorns in the fall. The best species on the East Coast is the white oak, which is comparatively sweet, and you can spot it by the rounded lobes on the leaves. Red oak has pointy leaves and a fuzzy coat around the acorn kernel and is relatively bitter. Huge twisty-limbed valley oaks proliferate in California. It's actually illegal to cut them down; in fact, there's one in my neighborhood growing in the street. Cork oak, which is exactly where cork comes from, is just okay. From some oaks it is practically impossible to remove the tannic bitterness, and in others they're nearly sweet right off the tree. There is a tree in the park across from my house that drops acorns that are sweet raw; nibbling on them one day I noticed a squirrel eyeing me with contempt and a few humans staring derisively. For most acorns, apart from tasting, there is only one way to tell: Shell and boil up a few and change the water several times. If they're still bitter, best to try another tree. Originally, acorns were just buried in mud for several months or soaked and then roasted. I like to think that people learned this trick from birds and squirrels—those they forgot about naturally sprouted and grew into trees. But let's try the grinding technology.

The acorns need to be thoroughly dry (a low oven for 1 or 2 days is fine, or store them for a few months or up to a year) and they must be without wormholes. If you are adventurous you can build a raised hut out of cedar, called a chuka, and line it with laurel to keep the bugs away. Bash open your dried acorns with a big rock (hitting them on the flat top of the acorn works well), then separate from the shells, or winnow them in a basket. Don't worry if you've broken them in the shelling process. Incidentally, you can use the little caps as a great whistle: With both hands, hold the open side of the cap underneath your parallel thumbs and tilt each thumb slightly outward until you form a little V-shaped opening just below your thumbnails. Put your thumb knuckles up to your lower lip and blow as hard as you can. If you get it right, it is piercingly loud.

After this bit of diversion, go to your grinding rock—this will be a depression in a large stone outside—with a round pestle, and grind the acorns into a fine powder. Next you must leach them of tannins. Dig a shallow depression in sand or find a finely woven basket. Put in your acorn meal and slowly pour over water, which will seep into the sand or through the basket, carrying away the bitterness. You'll need to do this over and over again until the meal is sweet. I've heard of people putting the acorn meal into a bag and setting it in a flowing river. The river near my office, the Calaveras, is pretty well polluted, so I haven't tried that. Or simply soak and drain the meal wrapped in a cloth set in a pot over and over again, or leave it under a running faucet.

The traditional way of cooking acorns is to fill a watertight basket with acorn meal and water, then heat up some hot volcanic rocks in a fire (the kind that don't explode, washed quickly by dipping into a bucket of water, once removed from the fire) and drop them right into the basket with the acorn meal and water. This makes a kind of porridge or nupa. It's stirred with a special stick that is looped at the end, with which you can remove the rocks. It takes about 20 minutes to cook through.

You can also make thick cakes by mixing the nupa into a dough with water and putting little rounds to bake in an earth oven. But if you've gone through this whole process, and are still unimpressed, try making crepes. The moist meal should be thoroughly dried into flour if you want to store it. Then proceed with the exact same recipe as on page 15 for wheat flour crepes. Even if you just use eggs, milk, and a little sugar alone, the result is tasty. Baking powder and vanilla seem out of place here, so the crepes will be a little brittle and rolling might be difficult. On the other hand, a drizzle of maple syrup seems perfectly appropriate, even if geographically improbable. The crepes are very dark, nutty, and quite delicious. You can also try making abelskivers from acorn flour, which are little round pancakes cooked in a special pan with hollow depressions. They are perfectly delightful with blackberry jam.

—K

Injera

The mother of all pancakes, and I don't mean this facetiously at all, is injera, one of the staples of Ethiopian cuisine. It is made of teff flour, a tiny grain that is nutty and really flavorful. Don't be tempted to use yeast, baking powder, or regular flour here. Just equal parts teff flour and water to start, mixed in a bowl. If you have heavily chlorinated water, use bottled spring water. Let the mixture sit out for a day. You'll see a dark sour-smelling liquid on top. Pour that off and add in fresh water to make a thin batter and stir. Repeat the next day, and then on the third day you should be ready to go, but don't pour off the water this time. Add a little salt at this point. Find the largest, flattest pan you have. Heat it and grease very lightly with oil. If you don't have a cover for this pan make a large tent out of foil by folding the ends of several sheets together so you have one big foil cover. Swirl in the batter with a ladle starting at the outer periphery. It shouldn't be as thin as a crepe, but not too thick, either. Cover with the foil and let cook—on one side only. You'll see little holes erupt on the upper surface. Carefully remove the injera, let it cool on a platter and continue with the rest of the batter. Traditionally you serve this on a platter piled with little mounds of stewed spicy chicken, lentil puree, and vegetable dishes. Extra injera is used torn, with the right hand only, to scoop up little parcels, and it is a sign of respect to feed your neighbors by popping these bundles directly into their mouths.

Completely untraditionally, this same lovely pliant chewy bread can be used to wrap other ingredients like a big rolled sandwich. Cold cuts, leftovers, jelly, tuna, dressed salad—all work well. It's a distant cousin of the blintz, of course. Just cut sections out of the roll, large or small.

—K

Paõ de Queijo

Paõ de queijo is based on tapioca flour (aka manioc or cassava). Actually it's a starch that can be bought from Brazilian suppliers; almost any Asian shop carries it, too, as it's used in many kinds of dumpling wrappers. For paõ de queijo boil 1 cup of milk and 4 tablespoons of butter with a pinch of salt. Gradually add 2 cups of the starch, and then add in 2 eggs and a handful of a fresh young cow's milk cheese. Farmer's cheese or queso fresco is nice, but so is pepper Jack or Cheddar. Cook briefly until amalgamated and thick. Let this cool, then knead. Coat your hands with starch and roll the dough into balls. You may need to add a little more tapioca. Place on a greased cookie sheet, or better yet in little muffin tins, and bake at 400°F for 20 to 30 minutes, until they've puffed up nicely and are a little browned. Popping them under the broiler works, too. Let them cool thoroughly before you eat them.

—K

Lefse

At the risk of making you dizzy from hopping around the globe, let's jump over to Norway for a flat potato bread. Start by making mashed potatoes, preferably with big mealy russets. Peel, cut the potatoes into equal-size pieces and boil them until just cooked through. Then pass them through a ricer or mash thoroughly as you please. Add butter and cream and some salt. Let this cool and add enough flour to make a stiff rollable dough. You can actually make gnocchi out of these at this point, too; just roll into little nubbins with your hands and boil. But for lefse you want a rolling pin and a lefse stick, which is a long flat stick. Our friend Paul from Minneapolis sent a beautiful one that replaced the wooden paint stirrer I was using. On a board covered with a well-floured pastry cloth, roll out a fist-size ball of dough into a thin circle. There are neat notched rolling pins that give your lefse an interesting woven pattern, but you can make the breads without one. Then slide your stick underneath the rolled-out dough, which will flop in half as you lift it. Match the edge of the lefse to the edge of a very hot flattop grill or pan, and then gently roll the whole thing over so the lefse and the cooking surface are aligned. No greasing is necessary. If you don't have a lefse stick, you can lift it with your fingers. When cooked on both sides, stack them, covered, until you've finished with all the dough. They can be eaten with butter and sugar, but I think they're more interesting with things like ham, liverwurst, gravlax, or sausages, for breakfast naturally. In Norway a smaller version made without butter is called lompe, which you can buy on the street wrapped around a hot dog: *pølse med lompe.*

—K

Whey Polenta

You don't even have to add cheese to polenta when it's been cooked in whey. It develops its own remarkably rich cheese flavor.

If you think ahead, soak the polenta in the whey overnight or a few hours ahead of time to speed up the cooking process. Make sure your polenta is very fresh; ground corn of any sort develops nasty bitter flavors when even slightly rancid.

Whisk 1 cup of polenta and some salt into 4 cups of whey in a large heavy-bottomed pot. Bring to a simmer, stirring constantly. Cook until the polenta starts pulling away from the edges of the pot. Pour into a buttered dish and cool until quite firm. Cut in ½-inch slices and fry in plenty of butter over medium heat until golden on both sides.

If you have to turn away from the stove for a moment and the polenta starts sticking to the bottom of the pot, just turn off the heat and put the lid on it for a few moments. The sticky parts will steam soft. In fact, if you're busy doing other things, you can cook the polenta this way. Bring it to a boil, cover, and turn off the heat for a few minutes. Repeat two or three times until the polenta is thick and all the grains are soft.

If you don't have whey, or even if you do, add 1 cup of grated Parmesan at the end of cooking. You can also throw in half a stick of butter or more, especially if you plan to serve it soft and warm like grits rather than fried.

—R

2

Fruits, Vegetables, Nuts, and Condiments

Fresh from the field, most produce requires precious little intervention to be delicious. If it even needs heat, you can just clean it, season it, and cook it: sauté, roast, or steam it with salt and some flavorful fat (butter, olive oil, tallow, bacon fat).

The trick, then, is to find ways to preserve produce that won't wholly destroy its soul. Modern-day canning methods rely on long cooking times to kill dangerous bacteria, with the side effect of preserving just the form, and not the flavor, of the produce. The notable exceptions are tomatoes, which become a whole new creature when cooked into sauce, and condiments (like jam and pickles), whose sugar and acid reduce the need for long canning times.

The other path—my favorite—is fermentation. Instead of killing off all the bacteria to preserve our food, we can encourage friendly bacteria and yeasts to take over. The result is not just preservation, but transformation.

In this chapter, we talk about some beautiful ways to serve fresh fruits and vegetables (including ginkgo and durian), as well as two distinct fermentation methods: direct lacto-fermentation and vinegar pickling with homemade vinegar.

We've also included some seemingly novel, but really old-fashioned, jam recipes, along with sweet and savory condiments ranging from pomegranate molasses to fermented soy sauce.

Stuffed Vegetables

The chefs of the Ottoman Empire, whom we have to thank for some of the finest dishes ever to emerge from a kitchen, were obsessed with stuffed vegetables, and Turks still are. My ancestors, who lived under the sultan for about 400 years, learned many of these recipes, and I figure it must be in my blood. Show me an eggplant, I want to stuff it. Even New World tomatoes, peppers, zucchini, and pumpkin. They're all fine sautéed, but presented whole and stuffed, they are objects of unparalleled dignity. You can fill them with ground lamb and vegetables, preferably laden with cinnamon and cumin, but even simple vegetable fillings are delicious. My favorite of late are the little baseball-size round zucchini. If you make zigzagged knife insertions halfway into the top, all the way around, the vegetable will come apart evenly and look gorgeous. Then with a small spoon or melon baller, remove the inside flesh, leaving just enough of the interior wall so it holds its shape. You can use a regular zucchini, too, cut horizontally the same way. Finely chop the flesh. Sauté it with olive oil in a pan with an onion, a little garlic if you like, and some aromatic herbs and spices. I like za'atar, which is a combination of thyme, oregano, sesame seeds, and sumac. Let this cool and then add some grated cheese or crumbled feta. You can stop there or add a few beaten eggs so the whole mix stays together. You may not have enough filling for all the shells, so feel free to add whatever other vegetable you have at hand, like mushrooms or chopped spinach. Then put the tops back on and bake the stuffed zucchini in the oven on medium heat for about 1 hour. This makes a great side dish or serve a few as a main course, breakfast, lunch, collation, late-night snack. You get the idea.

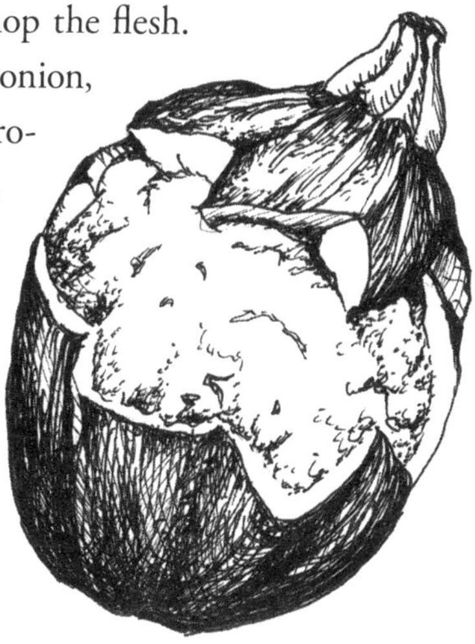

—K

Colcannon Ramped Up

Should you find yourself with a surfeit of esculent greens, colcannon is a sublime way to use them up. It's a stalwart Irish dish, served on Halloween with little coins concealed inside for the lucky children who find them without breaking their teeth. This version is not only much more interesting than the usual mashed potatoes and cabbage mix, but easier to cook. Start with a bunch of greens—turnips are best—along with 3 little turnip roots, 2 shallots, 1 potato (boiled and mashed coarsely), and a judicious amount of the finest slab bacon you can find cut into thick rashers, roughly chopped, and lightly cooked in a skillet to remove some of the fat (but not crispy). Save some of the fat in the pan. Leeks are also divine, or even better—as the section title suggests—ramps. Or use a plain old onion.

Chop the greens finely and put them in a pot. On top of these put the other vegetables, chopped. Then the bacon, then the mashed potato. Plus a little salt. Add 2 cups of water. You could use milk, but not necessary. Steam everything for about 10 minutes until soft and continue to cook with the lid removed to evaporate most of the water. Remove the mixture and place in the skillet in which you cooked the bacon. Stir often until dry and beginning to brown. Cook this as long as you like on low heat, just don't let it burn. This makes a whole meal unto itself, serve with a nice rich stout or porter. Butter is not necessary, but if you're feeling really indulgent, go ahead. And if you're feeling penitent, leave out the bacon and skip the pan-frying step. It's still scrumptious.

—K

Pickling

There are two basic species of pickle: those fermented with natural bacteria (*Lactobacillus* and a host of others) and those made with vinegar. I will admit to a prejudice against the latter, as somehow quick easy and, dare I say, fake. That describes most commercial pickles, pasteurized, mass manufactured, and sold in jars. They're very expensive, too, if you want something exciting like asparagus or okra pickles. I never really understood how delicious vinegar pickles could be until I started making them myself—with my own vinegar. So the idea is still bacterial fermentation, you are just letting the bacteria work on the fermented grape or grain first before adding the vegetables. There's nothing fake about it. And if you use store-bought, excellent-quality vinegar, they can still be quite lovely. I'm converted. But let's start with the vinegar.

Vinegar: The Mother

You can find vinegar recipes easily. One version is made from pineapple peels. It will eventually swarm with fruit flies, which it's supposed to do! Or someone may offer to give you a piece of *mother*, which is a rubbery snot-like raft that floats on top of homemade vinegar; it contains the *Acetobacter* that converts wine into sour wine, *vin-aigre*. People get obsessive about the mother. She has been cherished for six centuries, handed down from the Knights Templar; after their order was disbanded it was hidden in a Scottish monastery and passed on to the Rosicrucians and Free Masons.

Well, like bread and pickles and everything else wonderfully bacterial, vinegar makes itself. You just need to give it the right conditions. Maybe our problem is that we call it a mother and think it must be a thing that can't generate on its own. It can, with bacteria of course. The trick is, you need to make wine first. Most wine you buy contains sulfur, added precisely to stop fermentation and prevent it from ever turning into vinegar. I've seen store-bought wine go bad, but never turn into good vinegar.

I discovered this by accident to tell the truth. I had one large glass of homemade wine left over from a fall crush and just left it on a shelf and forgot about it. For about 3 months. When I rediscovered the wine, there was this slimy raft on top. Smelled like vinegar, tasted like vinegar. Eureka!

To start, crush organic grapes. (Who knows what is sprayed on conventional grapes to kill bacteria!) Whatever quantity you like. Whatever kind you like, too. Wine grapes work very nicely. Let them ferment in a capacious vessel exposed to the air, pushing down the floating peels and stuff on top every day, or more often. Bubble, bubble, toil, but no trouble. You will have made wine in 2 weeks or so. Strain out the solids. You don't need a press, just squeeze with your hands or wrap in a towel and twist it to get the last drops out.

Leave the liquid out, covered loosely, for about 3 months. Consider this your starter mother. At this point you can actually use whatever wine you like, just keep a crock going into which you can dump any dregs from leftover bottles or glasses. Or whatever alcohol, as long as it's roughly between 5 and 12 percent. The mother keeps renewing itself as you add more wine, so feel free to remove some and experiment with other types of vinegar. You can try beer: Just a few bottles with a chunk of the mother turns into a splendid malt vinegar. Rice wine also works nicely. Turning hard cider to vinegar seems to be a little more tricky, so I suggest making your own decent cider first from apples, leaving it out and letting it acidify.

Vinegar Pickles

Absolutely any vegetable you like can be pickled with vinegar, either white or red wine vinegar or any other type. Simply start with a strong brine, 4 or 5 percent salt, which is salty enough to float an egg. Mix in an equal part of your vinegar. Or use a greater proportion of vinegar. I usually find straight vinegar way too sour. Actually the best use for this is pickled eggs. Just hard boil them, peel, and toss in with spices, saffron if you like them yellow, a peeled beet if you want them red.

As for vegetables, hard ones like carrots and turnips should be cut to equal lengths and very briefly blanched. You want them crunchy and firm but not raw. The brief cooking begins to break down the cell walls. Start with string beans, they are the easiest. Just top and tail and throw in with dill fronds and a tiny touch of sugar. Maybe a chili pepper. Then move up to asparagus, okra (which can also be tossed in raw), cauliflower florets, and broccoli. Mix them together, too, however you like. Certain combinations are classic, like cauliflower, carrots, pearl onions, and peppers in an Italian giardiniera (or sottaceti). Rutabagas are magnificent pickled as are sliced beets. The flavorings are entirely up to you. Just avoid powdered spices or the whole thing will get cloudy. Try coriander seed, cumin, celery seed, cardamom, fennel, juniper berries, or peppercorns. Experiment; there is no way to ruin these. And most important, they do not need to be canned, processed, refrigerated, or anything. Just fill your jars and close the lid. I have kept jars for over a year on the shelf, and they actually improved with age.

The only thing you can do if you really want to ruin them is try smoking the vegetables first. They taste just like eating a sour cigarette butt. Well, I tried!

And if you have vegetables that demand immediate pickling, without the time to use your own vinegar, a good store-bought wine vinegar works well, too.

—K

Lacto-Fermented Pickles

With nothing but salt, water, and time, you can transform almost any firm vegetable into a puckered, sour version of itself. Salt kills off nasty putrescent bacteria, allowing friendly salt-loving bacteria to colonize the pickles. As these bacteria proliferate, they produce lactic acid, preserving the vegetables for long storage and giving them a wonderful sourness.

We cover quite a few fermented pickles in our first book, but we wanted to revisit the method here because it is so fundamental. Lacto-fermentation is quite simple and eminently versatile, as you might expect from a technology that's been preserving the produce of thousands of generations.

Start with any firm, fresh, clean produce: small cucumbers (of course), peppers, Brussels sprouts, cauliflower, hard green tomatoes, hard green baby watermelons, and so on. Place the cleaned and trimmed vegetables in a large jar or crock. Make a brine of about 2 tablespoons of salt per 1 quart of filtered water (no bacteria-killing chlorine, please), and pour it over the vegetables to cover them. Place a small plate or jar on top of the vegetables to keep them submerged under the brine, and use a rubber band to secure a napkin or other finely woven cloth over the mouth of the crock. You want air to circulate, but you do not want bugs to reach the pickles.

Leave the crock in a cupboard for a week or more. Check on it occasionally to remove any bits of mold that float on the surface (harmless, but it needs to go). The pickles are done when they taste pleasantly sour to you. The timing will depend on the warmth of the cupboard and the density of the vegetables. Brussels sprouts, for example, take a long time to get pickled all the way through. When your pickles are done, transfer them to a jar and store, sealed, in your refrigerator. They will keep for several months.

You can also add all sorts of delicious spices and herbs. Whole cloves of peeled garlic, peppercorns, coriander seeds, sprigs of dill, allspice, and juniper berries are all quite good, but play around. The salt level of the brine is also adjustable: the saltier it is, the slower the fermentation, but the longer the pickles will keep.

If your cucumber pickles get mushy, consider adding a few grape or oak leaves. One or two large leaves per quart will do. In my case, I have to run into Golden Gate Park for twigs from the coast live oaks, whose leaves are very small. I'll put half a dozen in a jar. The tannins in oak and grape leaves are what keep the pickles crisp.

—R

Using Brines, Pickles, and Whey

Making your own pickles and cheese can leave your refrigerator bursting with gallons of odd liquids. Sometimes the pickled vegetables themselves are even a bit perplexing—now that summer's bounty is sitting in your refrigerator, what can you *do* with it, besides nibbling it plain?

For starters, check out Effortless Sourdough Bread with Whey or Brine on page 5, Whey Polenta on page 22, and Pork and Sauerkraut on page 76.

Pickle Brine

Last summer I threw some small slightly spicy peppers into a brine with garlic and coriander. A few weeks later a pickly, peppery aroma filled my entire pantry, and the peppers were nicely pickled. They're quite delicious sliced on top of chili, for the record.

When I repacked the peppers from the original crock into jars for refrigerator storage, I found I had some extra brine. I couldn't bring myself to dump it because—although it took up precious space in my apartment-size refrigerator—I liked it *better* than the pickles. The brine was sweetly, aromatically peppery, savory, and complex. It was like pepper wine. I started using it as the base for all my salad dressings and whisked it like lemon juice into my mayonnaise and aioli.

The point is that homemade pickle brine can be used as a weak acid in your recipes. Think of it as an especially savory and aromatic diluted vinegar or lemon juice. Splash some in your soup just before serving. Marinate your meat in it.

Simplest of all, use a little pickle brine when starting your next batch of pickles. It will act like a starter, speeding up the proliferation of those wonderful lactic acid bacteria. Of course, this is only true for a raw, nonvinegar pickle brine.

Whey

When making cheese, the vast majority of the milk's volume turns into whey. There are a few delicious cheeses you can make from that whey—see ricotta and mysost, for example. But if you're not up for that, you will quickly find yourself shuffling around jars of the pale greenish liquid in your fridge.

Provided the whey itself is not salted (and most cheeses are salted after the whey drains out), you can also use the whey as a soup base or as the water replacement in bread. In fact, the lactic acid bacteria in the whey will give the bread an instant sourdough-like character, and the residual sugars in the whey will help your loaf brown beautifully. After soaking beans and draining off the soaking liquid, try cooking them in whey. Whey leaves everything it touches with a subtle sweet cheesiness.

I particularly like rolled oats soaked overnight in whey. I bring them to a boil first thing in the morning with a bit of cinnamon, salt, and butter, then turn off the heat immediately and let them steam, covered, for 15 to 20 minutes.

—R

Jams and Mostarda

Jam making is supposed to be an ordeal. You need several hundred pounds of fruit, dozens of canning jars, a 20-quart stockpot, tongs, packets of pectin, funnels. Wait, what did people do before Pasteur? Just cook down fruit and put it in any old sealed crock? Absolutely. And it will work if I want to use maybe a few pints of tiny *fraises des bois*, fresh raspberries from the farmer's market, or a little bag of juicy peaches. Or, best of all, gooseberries if you can find them. Scale is of no importance here at all. Rosanna offered some really superb and detailed directions in our first book together, and I have to admit, she started me on jam making. I am now prepared to wing it and so can you. In a nutshell: Throw fruit in pot. Toss on some sugar. Add in some lemon peel with the pith (the source of pectin). Boil until everything falls apart and the liquid gets thick. Remove the peel. Pass the mixture through a food mill if there are seeds (as with raspberries and strawberries). Put in jar hot. Seal. Done.

Now for the fun part. You can buy decent jam in any supermarket, but you can't buy serious spiced-up jam, or at least not just anywhere. Start by adding to your fruit base some finely chopped jalapeños or soaked anchos. This is stunning with cream cheese on crackers. Or add some crushed mustard seed. This is a variation on the Italian mostarda di frutta. Especially if you have sour fruit, the piquancy of the mustard sets it off so nicely. This goes with meat. Cinnamon and nutmeg also work wonders with cooked fruit. Just toss whole pieces in and fish them out toward the end if you like, or use ground spices. And just in case you think this is some outlandishly ridiculous novelty that no real Italian person would do, my friend Bartolomeo Scappi (chef to the popes in the mid-sixteenth century) made a red currant sauce, exactly as above, which was published in his Italian *Opera* (Works) of 1570. How about the one he calls *mostarda amabile* (lovely mustard)? The grape sauce he mentions is just cooked-down grapes with sugar, done the same as other fruits, and strained. Ironically the word *mustard* in English comes from the word for *grape juice* (must) and our modern condiment forgets the grapes and keeps the mustard seed. Here's the original version from Scappi (I really love his loose attitude):

> *Take one pound of grape sauce, and another of quinces cooked in wine with sugar, four ounces of apple cooked in wine, and sugar, three ounces of candied citron peel, two ounces of candied lemon peel, half an ounce of candied nutmeg, pound all together with the quince, and the apple with the mortar, and when everything is pounded pass it through a sieve together with the grape sauce, and add to this material three ounces of cleaned mustard, more or less depending on if you want it strong. And after straining add a little salt, finely pounded sugar, half an ounce of pounded cinnamon, and a quarter of pounded clove. And if you don't want to pound this mixture just break them up small. And if you don't have grape sauce, you can do it without, just use quince and apple cooked in the way mentioned above.*

Mustard

Mustard as we know it today, incidentally, is absolutely simple. Use a mixture of yellow and brown seeds. The surprising part is that it tastes acrid and bitter immediately after you make it, but if you leave it for a few days the bitterness dissipates. Also odd is that water activates the heat so you need to either soak your seeds first or grind them and add water. It doesn't matter if you soak first and then grind or grind and then soak. Either way, the seeds will absorb the water, and the longer they hydrate, the hotter they'll be. Once you've pounded the seeds, finely or coarsely, into a paste, then add flavorings such as vinegar, salt, a touch of honey or maple syrup is lovely, and a drizzle of beer or white wine works nicely. Throw in anything you like.

—K

Soy Sauce

Nowadays most soy sauce is made on an enormous industrial scale. That's not to say it's bad or even untraditional. The Japanese Kikkoman Corporation goes back to the seventeenth century, but every now and then you'll hear mention of some tiny artisan producer, making only a few cases that go for hundreds of dollars each. Well, why not try making your own? Here is the procedure. Mind you, this is a replication of the most primitive form of soy, called jiang, which originates in China. There are versions that use only soybeans; this one also includes wheat.

Boil a pound of whole red winter wheat (which you can find in the supermarket or online) until cooked thoroughly and soft, then pound it into a course wet meal in a really big mortar. Do the same to a pound of yellow soybeans. Then knead them together into a dough by hand, roll them into balls and put them in a big bowl on a bed of rice inoculated with the mold *Aspergillus oryzae*. This is sold in a little bucket, with rice and mold included, at most Japanese grocery stores. I have seen recipes that just allow any mold at all to settle in, but if it can be purchased, then why not use the right one?

Let this sit in a warm place, covered loosely with a cloth, until the whole thing is blanketed with a thick shag of white mold. Then toss the hairy balls into a strong brine (that's just water with a handful of salt) in a jar and put in the back of a cupboard and forget about it. Wait about a year, though you can always take a peek if you're impatient. When the contents of the jar are dark and fragrant, you'll need to devise a contraption to press the liquid out of the balls. Wrapping small batches of balls in several dishtowels and then placing under a weight works well. Be sure you set the batches on a tray to catch the liquid. Pour the liquid off periodically into a small bottle. It will be lighter in color than most soy sauce, which is darkened with caramel, and more pungent. Try it with a slab of raw fish or a vegetable. It would be a shame to cook with this, but of course you can. The leftover solids can be used just like miso paste, which is pretty much what it is. Stir it into a soup or flavor a sauce or marinade with it.

—K

Ginkgo Nuts

As a senior in college, I lived above Dupont Circle in Washington, DC, on Fifteenth and Swann, in a neighborhood that was then pretty much on the edge of upcoming and still fairly seedy. Today it seems to be pretty yuppified. The principal charm of the venue was the stately ginkgo trees lining the avenue. They were given by the ambassador from Japan in the late nineteenth century, when the houses were all built.

Since then, I have had an overwhelming affection for this species of tree. They've been around for twenty-five million years, living fossils. Male trees have motile sperm. They are closer to animals than to plants. And when the females bear fruit, you better believe it, the aroma is feral, but the leaves are so delicately beautiful, yellow maiden hair fans, it's worth the season of stench. Come that season, early in the morning, elderly Asian women are seen collecting the yellow fruits. So I thought, after years living with a beautiful tree right down the block, it was time to snatch a few from the ground and see what the fuss is about. Give it a try, and you'll find out for yourself.

My friend Willa, expert in such matters, told me, thank goodness, that you need to wear sturdy rubber gloves. Not just because of the stink, but the fruit around the nut is caustic. So don your gloves and collect them in a sturdy plastic shopping bag. Bring them into the backyard—for heaven's sake, don't do this inside! Wear a mask if you must. You've smelled durian before, right? Try a hundred times more potent. Peel away the fruit with your well-gloved fingers, but don't under any circumstances be tempted to taste the soft part. The stench alone will linger in your nostrils for days, but it's worth it. Wash the interior beige nuts many, many times with a hose *outside*. Use an old scrubby sponge, too. Then crack the nuts as gently as possible to remove the shells. The odor will still be dizzying. Soak the nuts in hot water briefly and peel off the dark papery skin beneath the shell. Then voilà! Tender, almost translucent greenish orbs. Edible poetry. Two hours of labor later, you will have a cup of nuts, if you're lucky. They're intriguing raw but better slightly toasted in a pan with a sprinkle of salt, which balances nicely with their inherent hint of bitterness. You can put them on a little skewer as Japanese yakitori. Or they're very nice in a stir-fry, too. You can, of course, buy them, usually canned, in an Asian market, but they just don't taste as good as when you've done it yourself and survived the purulent fecal onslaught.

—K

Durian

Speaking of durian, this is a large fearsome spiked beast of a fruit. If you live near a Southeast Asian grocery, they'll stock them. The impressive exterior is nothing compared to the bizarre creamy white custardy flesh that smells a little like armpit, a little like garlic, and a little like crap. It is, despite all this, remarkably delicious, the king of fruits in fact. It is meant to be hacked open and eaten, nothing more. But the texture is so reminiscent of custard, that freezing it is just irresistible. Just remove the seeds, puree the fruit with a little sugar and a splash of alcohol, which will prevent it from freezing solid. Then just pop it in the freezer and scrape out with a spoon. Tempt your friends with spoonfuls. Some will hate you for it, but the fortunate few will reel with delight.

—K

Pickled Green Walnuts

They say that stolen fruit tastes the best, as I learned one day after pilfering a few green walnuts from a neighbor's tree. I think the gods punished me well though: Without thinking I poked them all over with a pin, only to find that my hands had turned completely black and stayed that way for about 1 week. The lesson learned: Ask a friend first, and wear gloves.

Pickled green walnuts are traditionally made on June 24, St. John the Baptist's Day, when the walnuts are still soft inside and the shell hasn't formed yet. Poke them all around with a pin and put them into a pickle solution of half vinegar, half water, and a few tablespoons of salt. Flavor the mixture with a cinnamon stick, mace, and nutmeg and cloves, if you like. Any warm spices, plus plenty of peppercorns. Now forget about it. I mean, really, throw it in the back of a cabinet you rarely use. If you can wait a year, all the better. They will be blackened, sweet and sour, and remarkably complex. You eat the whole thing, preferably with something like a plowman's lunch: a wedge of cheese, an apple, some good ale, and maybe a slice of pork pie. Rare and intriguing is the only way to describe these.

—K

Pomegranate Molasses

My pomegranate molasses recipe is as simple as can be, but it yields a condiment that is not only unbelievably delicious but also lasts forever and is extremely versatile. Its origin, like the pomegranate, is the Middle East and the Mediterranean. Traditionally, this molasses is a souring agent in lamb stews or in marinades for chicken. It also goes really nicely with eggplant, but you can use it anywhere you want a deep sweet-and-sour flavor. Put a spoonful into a tomato sauce or even into ground beef for hamburgers. No one really knows it's there, but eyebrows are raised.

Get a large quantity of pomegranates. I was given a big shopping bag by my pal Luigi who has a tree, so I couldn't imagine eating them all. Actually I have a little tree, but it's never borne fruit. Anyway, break them open with your hands. It will, unfortunately, look like someone has been murdered after you're done.

Strip back the red peel and the bitter white peel and put only the red seeds into a stockpot. Don't worry if you break a lot in the process, just make sure you don't leave any white pith in the pot.

Then cook the seeds down with a few tablespoons of unrefined sugar and a vanilla pod. After the seeds have all broken down, strain the liquid and return it to the pot. Keep the vanilla pod in with the juice. Keep the liquid on a very low simmer for about 3 hours until reduced. In the end you'll have a lovely, tart, nutty sweet, blood-like super-thick syrup. About a dozen pomegranates will give you a couple of cups at most, which is fine. You'll need only a spoonful at a time. You can stir a spoonful into ice water for a refreshing and antioxidant drink that won't set you back five bucks. And just in case you don't have a costume for Halloween, use this syrup and go as your favorite saint, dripping blood from some missing body part. This would be great for Lucy without her eyes, or even better, Oedipus.

—K

Carob Molasses

Carob is one of those health foods that suddenly appeared on the market when I was a kid, as a substitute for chocolate, which it isn't. If you think of it rather as a kind of dark sweet fruity pod to gnaw on, it's much more palatable. There's a huge tree across the street from my office, and I am often seen snatching a few pods to bring to class for show-and-tell. It is supposedly what St. John ate in the desert as locust beans. Its seeds are also the origin of the carat from Greek *keration*, used as a measure of weight for gemstones. Most interesting of all, a syrup is made from carob throughout the Middle East called gulepp tal-harrub, which is used in cooking; on the island of Malta it's made into a drink with water. To make the syrup, just break up the pods, boil them for several hours in water and then strain. Cook this down until thick, adding a little sugar to taste if you want. In a barbecue sauce or chili it is really haunting.

—K

Sanct Johansbern-Suppen

I spent one summer doing research in the gorgeous little town of Wolfenbüttel in lower Saxony at the Herzog August Bibliotek. It is an absolute gem of a library. I was actually accidentally locked in one weekend when the library closed early and seriously considered staying there until Monday. I ended up climbing up a bookshelf and jumping out a window next to a group of alarmed tourists, fully expecting to be pursued. Anyway, you can imagine my delight to discover not only that there was a press there for a few years but that in 1598 they published a cookbook: *Kunstbuch von Mancherley Essen* by Frantz von Rontzier. In it there are three versions of a soup called sanct johansbern-suppen; the following is a compromise among the three. We rarely think of using fruit in a soup nowadays, let alone using the even rarer red currant. But this is so remarkably fresh and bracingly sour, that it makes an ideal opening to a meal, a custom that is well worth reviving.

Take red currants and sauté them gently in butter. Add some

wine (dry rosé is best), and simmer until they are softened but not disintegrated. Place a slice of toast in a shallow soup dish, pour the soup over and sprinkle mace, cinnamon, and a little sugar on top. You can also add a little rose water. Although this is intended to be eaten hot, it is also very nice chilled.

—K

3

Meats

We are not contrary people by nature but find it very hard to heed warnings to limit, or heaven forfend curtail entirely, our consumption of succulent morsels of tender flesh. Would life be worth living without bacon, cold cuts, sausages, hearty stews, and mouthwatering roasts? We think not. We know there are like-minded folk out there who obsess about such things as much as we do; some go so far as to wield the cleaver and saw, butchering their own meat. We salute you all. Good meat, we are all coming to appreciate, comes from well-reared animals that have lived full and, dare I say, *happy* lives. So for all the following recipes, do source your ingredients as best you can and be sure that the life that was given to sustain your own was not sacrificed in vain.

Weight Watcher's Veal

My mother's penchant for contriving strange dishes was proverbial. It might have been peas and raisins in a salad or maybe flounder cooked in the dishwasher. Or the "just like fresh" objects drawn from the freezer at the slightest hint that someone might be hungry.

So it was with no small measure of apprehension when, twenty years ago, she invited my new girlfriend to dinner. Mind you, this was during the week, and that meant that we would be eating at home because my parents were avid workday weight watchers. The situation was complicated by the fact that I'd had a string of strange girlfriends in years prior: an athletics coach from northern England with an inscrutable accent, a mad Las Vegas playwright obsessed with Armageddon, and a few others I have blocked out. In each case, the crucial first meeting and meal was fraught with anxiety for one simple reason—none of these women was Jewish. So I knew this one, my latest catch, would be treated differently, as the keeper and someone my mother would go out of her way to impress. That meant something special and home cooked.

My mother chose one of her signature dishes, something my father apparently liked, or never claimed otherwise. It was a dish I had come to dread. This night was to be a cozy supper for four of Weight Watcher's Veal, as she called it.

This is how I recall the dish being made: Obtain 1 pound of ground veal. Place it in a tepid pan without any oil until it oozes its liquid and boils. Cook until a grayish mass. Then add a packet of Lipton's onion soup mix. Add in a can of tomato paste, followed by enough water to make it vaguely chili-like. The key to the dish is that it then has to be cooked for several hours on the stovetop, loosely covered so its odors permeate the entire neighborhood. At the last minute, add a can of sliced button mushrooms, only partially drained to preserve the flavor of the can. Garnish with something like mandarin orange slices or pineapple rings. It is best served with converted rice.

Now when this dish appeared on the kitchen table (not dining room, presumably to lend an air of homeyness) all I can recall is my girlfriend's jaw dropping as she watched the pale and lurid mass being doled onto the plate. That she actually managed to get it down, out of politeness, was a minor miracle, as was the fact that she married me anyway.

This is how I make a pretty similar dish today: Take 1 pound of pork shoulder (aka country ribs) and coarsely chop by hand. Season with salt, pepper, oregano, and ground cumin. Heat a pan until extremely hot, pour in some olive oil and immediately place in the pork without stirring. It will smoke. Only when it is brown on one side and a nice fond has been created should you stir. Add in 1 finely chopped onion and let it brown. Lower the heat, and add a few cups of dry white wine to deglaze and a drizzle of vinegar.

Next take 2 dried mulato or ancho chilies and toast in a dry skillet. Then put them in a mortar with 1 cup of hot water. Let sit for 10 minutes, then pound into a fine paste. (Or blend if you must.) Add this to the simmering meat. Let cook for about 20 minutes, and then add about 1 cup of cooked kidney beans—or better yet teparies, my favorite. Then add 1 cup of hominy—nixtamalized whole white corn kernels. (You can make this yourself from field corn soaked in lye or calcium hydroxide or buy it canned.) If you like, a square of really good dark chocolate melted in will make this dish sing. Continue to cook very gently to let the flavors meld. Add a little water if it gets too dry. Serve with a crumble of queso fresco, some chopped tomato, and a few sprigs of cilantro.

—K

Pottage of Fat Goose with Pureed Peas

If you perchance peruse historic goose recipes, going much farther back than Dickens's roast goose served on the Cratchits' Christmas table, you will find a panoply of intriguing techniques. There is goose baked whole in a pastry crust in sixteenth-century Italy; goose stuffed with oats and boiled; goose semiroasted, slashed, and finished on the grill to make what was known as a *carbonado* in Restoration England; goose ragouts; and goose served in a staggering variety of sauces. But one in particular caught my attention. It hails from *Le Cuisiner* of Pierre de Lune, published in Paris in 1656, and involves salted-cured goose, served in a pottage of pureed peas. Here is the recipe, translated from the original:

Potage D'oie Grasse Aux Pois Passés

If the goose is salted, do not lard it; if it is not, then lard it with bacon; then cook it in a pan with lard, and then cook through with bouillon, and a bundle (of herbs). Cook your peas separately and pass through a sieve with the goose bouillon, parsley, a bit of pepper, and a morsel of green citron. Garnish with fried bread and little bits of crumbled bacon.

To help you re-create this dish, here is a full description of the technique. Carefully remove each breast half from the goose with a sharp boning knife. Keep the skin attached. Remove the legs and thighs intact for another use, such as confit. Use the bones and giblets for a light stock, which you can freeze for use later in the recipe. (Reserve the liver for yourself, seared and served on crackers.)

Mix 2 tablespoons of fine sea salt with 1½ tablespoons of unrefined sugar, ½ teaspoon of Insta Cure No. 1 (or pink salt, which can be bought online or at specialty grocers), 1 tablespoon ground pepper, and 1 tablespoon of crushed juniper berries. Liberally coat the breasts, put into a large gallon-size zip-closing plastic bag, and store in the refrigerator for 7 to 10 days. Turn the bag over every day.

Remove the breasts from the fridge, rinse off and pat dry. Brown them gently in a pan with 2 tablespoons of melted lard (or goose fat). Toss in a bouquet garni tied with string. Pour over goose stock to cover halfway and cook the breasts through very gently, with the pan covered, 15 to 20 minutes. The final texture and taste will be remarkably like cooked ham.

Meanwhile boil a pound of green or yellow split peas in the bouillon with some parsley, pepper, and candied green citron. Pass through a sieve or puree in a blender or food processor. To serve, put the peas, which should be fairly thick, in a large deep platter and lay the goose breasts, thinly sliced, on top. Scatter croutons and bits of crumbled bacon on top for garnish. Serves 4 to 6 people.

—K

Pickled Pig's Feet

E-bone and Mookie, my two sons, and I have some extremely silly rituals. Among these is going to pay our respects to the pickled pig's feet at the supermarket. They sit on the top shelf, aisle six, above the Spam display. In a big glass jar float little pink nubbins of gnarly flesh, skin, and fat. They look absolutely vile. I take the jar down (I'm certain it's the only one that has ever existed) greet it warmly, consider buying it for a split second, and always put it back. Why I am at once compelled to strike a cordial friendship with the feet but also long to taste them, I can't explain. It's not a weird-food machismo sort of thing because I love every part of the pig unabashedly.

Who eats these anyway? I'm fairly certain it's a southern dish, ultimately German. But the Irish, too, have their crubeens; think of the song "Galway Races" and "a big crubeen for thruppence to be pickin' while you're able," but I have never been able to find them in Ireland. The English, too, once loved their pig's pettitoes and I have cooked some historic recipes with miserable results. So maybe it was a just a challenge. The easiest place to find pig's feet is at an Asian supermarket.

Wherever you find yours, they should be split and cross-sectioned. Every pig comes with four trotters, right? They must be somewhere. Simmer them in a pot of water with aromatics such as celery, carrot, onion, and bay leaf until tender, 1 to 2 hours. Then put them in a jar, cover halfway with the simmering broth and half with white vinegar. Add a good handful of salt, some pepper, maybe a bay leaf, sage, coriander seeds, even a chili pepper wouldn't hurt. Cover the jar and leave it right out on the counter, as I am told was common practice in groceries throughout the South, right there next to the pickled eggs. Let the feet pickle a month or so. The flavor is truly intriguing: sour, piggy, fatty. It's surprising that they're not tough but really soft and tender, especially the skin. The brining liquid gels as well, even at room temperature. There is not much meat on them, but they're quite tasty. Not at all the chewy old foot you might expect. The idea of nibbling away at toes can be arresting, but it's good.

—K

Boudin Noir

I went for a ride one day, an aimless jaunt driven by boredom, and found myself at a huge newly remodeled Southeast Asian supermarket. I wandered around, looking for nothing in particular, pretending not to notice the intriguing aromas. I saw some very nice-looking produce, big bags of rice, live fish in tanks. And then, there it was. My heart's desire. Slightly stained, dripping a bit, but exactly what I've always been looking for. A *bucket* of blood. Five pounds of blood for $6. I bought a slab of pork belly and screwed up my courage to make some real boudin noir. Aka black pudding, alias morcilla. Whatever you call it, it's blood in a casing. Of course I imagined the bucket spilling in the car on the way home and getting stopped by a policeman: "Trust me officer, it's really just pig's blood!"

The procedure could not be more simple, if, that is, you can get past the bizarre gelatinous mass of congealed blood in the bucket. Here's how. This is a recipe that avoids fillers to maximize the full flavor of blood, which is absolutely delicious. Around the world you will find similar recipes that extend the blood with oats, breadcrumbs, and rice. Do as you please.

Take 2 pounds of very finely chopped pork belly, which is, like bacon, more than half fat, so the final mix should be a fifth fat, or 20 percent. To this you will add about 3 pounds of blood. You can squish it all up with your fingers to get it back to liquid state or, if you're squeamish, use an immersion blender. Add 1 teaspoon of Insta Cure No. 1 (that's the brand name for a salt and sodium nitrite mix), 3 tablespoons salt, a lot of pepper, even more nutmeg (which I adore), some thyme, and about 1 cup of shallots fried in fat. Pour the mixture through a funnel into the casings. You'll get about five foot-long puddings if you use beef middles. Poach these very gently in a big stockpot for about 25 minutes. At this point you can refrigerate or freeze them. A

lovely variation on the recipe is to add pine nuts and raisins, and a touch of chocolate and a pinch of sugar. The sweetness is surprisingly fetching.

When ready to serve, sauté them whole in a pan first. I find it best halfway through cooking to cut each pudding into rounds and sauté them so the sides get brown and crispy. You can serve with Granny Smith apples cooked right in the same pan. I will not hesitate to tell you, even at the risk of boasting, that this is the best boudin noir I have ever tasted. If you serve them with a fried egg, a roasted tomato, some mushrooms, fried bread, and rashers of bacon, you will understand that of which true bliss consists.

—K

Liverwurst

As long as we're stuffing casings, here's something just as easy to make and really delicious. You'll never get the very fine texture of store-bought liverwurst unless you use a lot more fat and have a machine that can pulverize it into an extremely fine paste. This is a little more rustic but tastes lovely. Start with a pig's liver. Yes it is disgusting. The ancients thought liver was just congealed blood because it was believed to be the organ that makes blood. They also thought that human livers have five lobes, but they were actually looking at pigs' livers. Anatomy lesson aside. Poach your liver in water until pale and firm. The pig's liver, not your own, though if you yourself go pale, remain firm and continue. Fry up an onion and add to the liver. Finely dice either pork fat and shoulder or pork belly. You want about equal measures of poached liver, meat, and fat—all well chilled. If you add a little more fat, that's fine. Season with spices and add salt. If the total measure is about 5 pounds, add 3 to 4 tablespoons. Now obliterate this into the finest puree you can, however you can. I use a monster mortar, but batches in a food processor would work fine I'm sure. Fill your casings and tie with string. Let rest several hours until the surface is a little tacky. Then smoke over smoldering oak logs (hot smoke) for about 2 hours. This is very simple, just light a wood fire in a smoker or even a small kettle-shaped portable barbecue grill, just until the wood is on fire, then cover it so the flames go out. Put in your wurst and let them smoke. Then let them mellow in the fridge for a few days. The interior will be fairly soft and spreadable. On a slice of dark pumpernickel, it is perfectly ethereal. A cold glass of beer is required.

—K

Coteghino

Here's another truly remarkable recipe to try, coteghino, also spelled cotechino, from Modena in Italy, which is made predominantly from pig's skin. You've likely tasted cracklings or chicharrones (*ciccioli* in Italian) or, as I like to call them, "fried football." Just imagine that same lovely flavor but in a soft yielding sausage. You can stuff these into a very fat casing, about the size of a small football, or into a hollowed-out pig's foot, in which case it becomes a zampone. Not Zamboni, that's what they use to smooth ice skating rinks, though a zampone might work, too. Imagine you are making a regular sausage, part meat and a bit of fat, but to maybe half of this standard mix, you add finely chopped raw pork rind. You can use a pinch of nitrate if you want for that lovely pink color. Season vigorously with herbs like sage or oregano and add some spice. Nutmeg is nice, and I like a hint of clove. Salt and pepper, too, of course. A dash of wine is good. Stuff and tie up your sausages and let the flavors meld for a few days in the fridge. Then gently boil your coteghino for 3 to 4 hours. Be sure to poke a few holes in it. If you like, you can make a bollito misto by adding a hunk of beef, a chicken, a tongue, and whatever else strikes your fancy to the boil. Eat with some mustard on the side and some green sauce made with parsley, garlic, oil and vinegar, thickened with breadcrumbs. Serve with lentils as a traditional side dish for New Year's Day, when the whole thing is sure to wake you up and cure even the worst hangover. Slice your coteghino before service, and eat it while hot.

—K

Pig Jam

I suppose the closest thing to pig jam that is actually eaten somewhere would be rillettes, which is basically just pork cooked for hours until it becomes stringy, with a lot of congealed fat, stored in a jar. The first time I had it was with breakfast while honeymooning in the Loire Valley. Oinktuous, spreadable goodness. (The fat serves as oinkment!) The version I offer here is very different and is really much more of a soft sausage stored in a jar rather than in a casing. The currently popular 'nduja is a relative, though that's actually in a casing, but soft and spreadable and wonderfully spicy. There are actually two versions of this recipe, one is raw and long cured, much like a salami, the other is very gently poached in a canning jar and comes out more like Spam, to tell the truth, or a soft breakfast sausage cousin of scrapple. They're all close cousins, so I would say play with this recipe until you find the one you like. What is nice is you can put it in really small jam jars and then open one for breakfast. It's also something you can make in a small batch, and you don't need any special equipment at all.

Start with 2½ pounds of fatty pork shoulder. Chop finely with 2 tablespoons sea salt, 2 tablespoons raw sugar or maple sugar, ⅛ teaspoon of Insta Cure No. 2 if you will do the uncooked version, or Insta Cure No. 1 for the cooked. These are nitrate mixes you can buy online. Add in flavorings like fennel seed, mustard seed, pepper, and sage. Entirely up to you. The trick here is you need a big stone mortar and you want to pound the ingredients very, very finely. It's something like making mortadella, another cousin. It will take a while. (A food processor will probably work, too.) While pounding toss in 3 ice cubes, one at a time, every couple of minutes. You'll see the mix turn into a kind of thick meat batter. Spoon into little jars. If doing the raw long cure, top with some melted lard and seal. Let sit 2 to 3 months in a cool dark place. For the quicker and cooked version, put the jars in a pot with a few inches of water and then poach for about 5 minutes. Turn the jars over and poach gently another 5 minutes. Remove them and turn upside down and let cool. The gelatinous broth and fat will settle at the top of the jar and create a seal. To serve give each person his or her own little jar, a knife, and some crusty bread with a few fried eggs.

You can also brown these in a pan—just turn out of the jar and fry up, if you prefer them hot. Or slice into rounds if you're using bigger jars.

—K

Beef Rindsrouladen

Beef, quite frankly, is among the most boring of meats. Unless you find a really well-aged steak, beautifully marbled with fat, quickly seared on a grill, and served extra rare, or as I say, *still mooing*, most beef is just pretty dull. Often the more expensive, the less interesting as well. Filet mignon is so soft and bland, more like baby food than meat. All the more reason to buy the cheapest cut and do something fun with it. The basic outlines of this recipe for Rindsrouladen come from my dear friend Melissa, who got it from her German grandmother. I like the idea of passing down the wisdom of the ancients, but I also like messing with things, though this is close.

Start with an inexpensive cut meant to be braised. Bottom round or top round is best, which is basically the steer's rear end. Flank or London broil should work well, too, but definitely not a steak. Carefully butterfly the meat horizontally and open it like a book; if you're able, cut both sides again horizontally from the center to the edges, so you have one long thin surface of meat, four times longer than the original. Pound it flat with a batticarne or flat-ended mallet. If you like, you can also make four smaller rolls. I just like the drama of one big one.

Salt and pepper the meat. Spread the top side with good

grainy brown mustard. Then a layer of chopped raw bacon; 4 slices should be enough. Then a sliced onion, then a couple of finely chopped sour dill pickles. (Ideally the bacon, mustard, and pickles will be your own homemade.) Carefully roll the entire thing up tightly and tie with string three or four times around and perhaps a few times across the length. You want to keep all that good stuff inside.

Lightly dust the roll in flour and in a capacious pan, brown the roll on all sides in oil. Then add some good beef broth and red wine (though beer would be great, too) to come up halfway on the roll. Throw in a bay leaf and some thyme tied up in a bundle. Braise gently, covered for about 1½ hours, or longer. You can even make this a day ahead, put in the fridge, and reheat the next day, it will be even nicer. When ready to serve, slice the meat, revealing the spiral of ingredients, and serve in a shallow dish in a pool of the gravy. Potato pancakes go wonderfully, as does spaetzle.

If you really want to mess with this recipe, feel free to borrow a trick from its relative, the sauerbraten, which is basically the same cut of beef, left whole; marinated in spices, vinegar, wine, and vegetables for a few days; then braised. The rolled-up meat bundle can also be marinated the same way. Before serving, crush a few gingersnap cookies into the gravy. Purists will declare this hybrid heresy, but the extra sour, spicy punch makes the rouladen doubly interesting. Or lean southward for another fun variant: Load the roll with capers, pancetta, and Mediterranean herbs. Use a dry white wine, a little tomato puree, and some cream or milk in the braise.

These kind of rolled-up meat braises have a long pedigree, and if someone suggests your variant is a mishmash without historical precedent, point them to sixteenth-century maestro Bartolomeo Scappi's magnificent recipe for brisavoli, which is slices of beef stuffed with pork fat, prosciutto, garlic, egg yolks, cheese, pepper, cinnamon, parsley, mint, and thyme. These are quickly roasted on a spit then simmered in a broth with grape syrup, agresto (the juice of unripe grapes), and raisins. Resplendent!

—K

The Celery Cure for Salumi

This is a true story, and I haven't changed the names to protect the innocent. One day I was sitting in a factory in Berkeley at the feet of Paul Bertolli, arguably the finest maker of organic salame in the country, learning about the technique as an absolute neophyte while working on *The Lost Art of Real Cooking*. He was a gracious host, generous with details, offering tastes, explaining the importance of well-reared pigs. I have nothing but respect for him. Then at one point I asked about nitrates, and he turned to me and said "No nitrates!" but, but . . . "No nitrates!!" He repeated. I finally coaxed out of him the secret of celery powder and how, for some reason, to qualify as organic, cured meats must contain no industrially produced nitrates, but celery powder is okay.

At that point, the major manufacturers of so-called no-nitrates cured meat said nothing about celery powder, it was just one among many natural flavorings. In effect, people were being lied to because celery powder does in fact contain nitrates, chemically indistinguishable from the industrial sodium nitrite. Since then, some companies, like Niman Ranch, do explain on the package that their bacon, franks, and other such products do contain nitrates naturally occurring in celery powder. But many people still believe they can buy cured meats that are nitrate free. You can't, there is no such thing. Even fat back salted and smoked tastes and cooks up very differently from bacon. Even if it says *uncured*, it's cured with celery powder.

In any case, you can easily find this celery powder cure online now. For short cures, it works fine: on sausages, bacon, pancetta. I've used it on everything, in the exact same proportions as Insta Cure, which is 1 teaspoon to 5 pounds of meat. I've used beef and pork and even goose breast, and I have to admit, I can't tell the difference. Where I don't think it really measures up is in long-dried and fermented products such as hard salami and bresaola. It doesn't have the double whammy of Insta Cure No. 2, a combination of sodium nitrite that kicks in immediately, plus sodium nitrate that slowly converts to nitrite. But ultimately if it is the chemical equivalent of Insta Cure No. 1, why bother?

The bigger question, however, is how European manufacturers claim to use no nitrates whatsoever. Either they are lying, are uninformed about what they are throwing in (which seems unlikely), or they are using locally mined salts that naturally contain nitrates. I have a feeling that's how it happened in the past, before you could buy the cure ready made. There are recipes that call for saltpeter (potassium nitrate) going back to the Middle Ages (in fact a whole deer preserved and buried!), but recipes don't regularly call for it until the nineteenth century. I think before then it was just already in the caves where they mined salt.

Regardless of which cure you use, here's a delightful little snack I first saw one Christmas in Brussels. Let's call them salami olives. Start with about 2½ pounds of pork shoulder, nice and fatty, and chop it very finely by hand. Add in 2 tablespoons of sea salt and 2 tablespoons of fine sugar. Maple sugar works really nicely, too, if you can find it. Add ½ teaspoon of cure and whatever seasonings you like—oregano, pepper, fennel, chili flakes, etc. Mix well by hand. Get very narrow-diameter casings, rinse them out well. Narrow hog casings are fine, about 1¼ inch in diameter. Tie off the end of the casing with string, and push it onto the tip of a funnel, then stuff the meat through the funnel into the casing, carefully pushing down the chopped meat. Poking a few pinholes in the casing makes it easier, but don't stuff it too tightly. Now the fun part—tie off the sausage at about 1-inch intervals, forming little olive shapes. (Some people just twist them, but I find they usually unravel.) Poke them all around with a pin. Let these cure in a cool, moist chamber for 1 or 2 months. Don't let them dry out too much or they become rock hard. When ready to serve, break off the olives and discard the strings. Put in a bowl next to regular olives. They're lovely to just pop in your mouth.

—K

A Note on Casings: From Sheep to Beef Bungs

Every time I buy sausage casings online, something quite different arrives in a white plastic bucket. Some are thin and delicate with a tiny diameter suitable for hot dogs or small breakfast sausages, such as the sheep casing. Some are massive. The beef bung is in the latter category. It is technically the caecum of a cow, one of the many stomachs found in ruminants. (We have a tiny one, too—the appendix.) Perhaps the most disconcerting part of this particular anatomical object is that it's closed on one end, a "blind gut" or cul-de-sac in French. In Latin, ancient Roman agricultural writers call it a fundolus, or dead end. It's just a big bag, maybe 5 inches in diameter, so you can actually just stuff it by the handful. It will easily hold 7 pounds of meat or more, so it may be best to tie off into smaller salamis, though it's the traditional casing for massive mortadella and the like. The nicest part about this size is that not only can it be cut into perfect sandwich slices but the curing takes much longer, at least 3 months, and you get a far more pronounced sour flavor from the natural bacteria. Just make sure you keep it somewhere cool, about 55°F and humid. Otherwise the outside will dry hard and the inside will remain soft, something known as *case hardening*. Also, be sure to tie this well as it will need support beyond a string at the top. The best way is to tie four or five strings from top to bottom. Then weave in as many strings as you need around the salami, tying them into the longer strings as you go around, and knotting tightly. As the salami dries, the strings will become loose and you may need to retie them or tighten them up.

Back to casings—there are also beef middles, which are used to make the classic long salami shape, about 2½ inches around, also easy to stuff by hand without a funnel. I have found that these tend to dry out quicker than other casings. There are also hog middles, about the same size, though I got some once that seemed much wider, with perfectly baroque folds and twists. They're quite thick and good for sopressata. Just be forewarned, they really stink. Exactly like what you might guess.

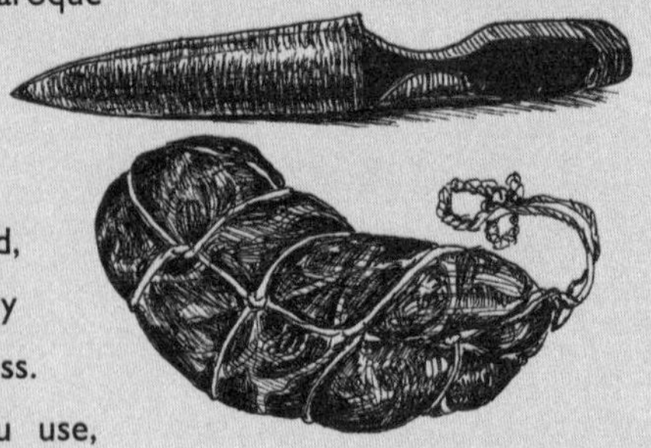

Whatever size you use,

while it's curing give the salami a little squeeze every now and then. You want it somewhere between soft and rock hard, entirely up to you though. As far as the contents go, I would encourage you to experiment. For example, some cayenne or ancho chili powder with cumin and garlic will give you a nice chorizo. Some soy, Shaoxing rice wine and ginger yields very nice lap cheong. Just be sure to use part salt and part soy sauce, as a too-liquid mixture will not dry well. Crushed juniper berries with maple sugar is my favorite, but again, try sage or tarragon and a splash of sherry, anything goes. As long as you keep to the basic proportions of 5 pounds of meat with about 20 percent fat, 3 to 4 tablespoons of salt, 3 to 4 tablespoons of sugar, and 1 teaspoon of Insta Cure No. 2, you should be fine. (I say 3 to 4 tablespoons because I just pour these into my palm.)

—K

Salam D'la Duja

Here is a remarkable way to cure salami, common in the Piedmont region of northwest Italy. The humidity makes traditional drying difficult, so the links are stored in a glazed earthenware vase (*duja*) and covered with rendered fat. After about 3 months, they are cured and sour, still a little soft, and disconcertingly for some people, still look raw. They aren't at all. Like the previously mentioned little salami olives, you can just pull one out of the pot and leave the rest. The important thing is not to put the crock in the refrigerator. If it's too cold, the meat will go bad rather than cure with good bacteria. The shelf is not a good idea either if you live in a very hot place. Somewhere cool, 55° to

60°F is ideal. The flavoring for these is traditionally just black pepper, but cayenne pepper goes so nicely, and it is reminiscent of the better-known 'nduja of Calabria, the name of which is said to be a version of the French andouille. It is pronounced the same way, too: *n doo ya*, but the two products are not even vaguely similar. I suspect there is no relation between this Piedmontese duja and the Calabrian 'nduja, either.

—K

Salo

I was told by my friend Katrina that in Ukraine, whence her ancestors came, they are obsessed with a kind of cured fat eaten in huge slabs on a hunk of bread. This is not delicate slices of Tuscan lardo cured in cool marble coffins. Nope, this is just wads of pig fat. I love the idea. So, with nothing more than a thick slab of pork leg fat, salt it with a little pink curing salt and sugar, and hang it up somewhere cool and damp. No casing is required, just tie it with string. Wait about a month. It is still very obviously just fat, but delicious, tender, and great on bread with a shot of vodka or two. You can also take it to another level by seasoning it well with sage and thyme and letting it cure just a few weeks. Then cold smoke it for several hours over apple-wood. Cold smoking is a little tricky: Basically you want a big chamber with a smoldering log inside, without letting the temperature get hot, which of course would melt the fat. It is so lovely, sliced on toast, you may never need bacon again.

—K

Stock

Making a good stock is quite straightforward: Put various animal bones in a pot, cover them with water, and gently, gently simmer them as long as you can.

Which bones to use? Anytime you eat flesh on the bone, save all the bones in your freezer. Every week or two, turn your collection into stock. Even the bones from a four-hour stew will still have plenty of goodness in them (especially if they are thick bones). If you can find some, add knucklebones to your stockpot, chicken feet if it's a poultry stock, or fish heads and shrimp shells for a fish stock. Heavy bones would be worth cracking or sawing into, if they come to you intact. The only bones you should not use are the bones of oily fish like salmon or sardines—their fragile polyunsaturated oils will quickly turn rancid when cooked, and very little could coerce you into tasting the stock.

Vegetables enrich a stock but aren't strictly necessary if you won't be serving it plain as broth. Save your onion and celery ends and carrot trimmings in a bowl in the fridge, and add them to your weekly stockpot.

You can also use fresh bony cuts of meat, like chicken legs, beef, or lamb neck bones or shanks, but you should remove the meat from the bones as soon as it is properly tender—an hour or less for birds, a few hours for red meat. Extended cooking in that much water will make the meat stringy and watery, and it won't contribute much to the stock. Shank bones have lots of delicious marrow inside—this should be scooped out after 20 to 30 minutes or so of simmering and eaten with a sprinkle of salt on toast, or a spoon. Return the bones to the pot, and keep simmering the stock.

Try to stack the bones closely in the pot, so you can cover them with the minimal amount of water. Poultry carcasses should be flattened. This will help your stock be very concentrated without extensive boiling later on. A little acid hastens the extraction of minerals and gelatin from the bones—add a splash of apple cider vinegar.

Poultry bones will produce a nice stock within a few hours, but you might as well leach out all the goodness and let them go overnight. More than a day, and the oils will go rancid and impart a nasty flavor to the stock. Beef and other large bones can simmer for 2 to 3 days, and the stock will only improve (more than a few days, and again, you'll face the issue of the fats oxidizing). By the time your stock is done, all the gristly cartilaginoid bits should be very tender—and delectable. Remove the bones and chill the stock.

If your bones are producing a great deal of fat, you would be wise to pause the stock halfway through cooking, chill it, and scoop the hardened fat from the surface. Save it, of course! This way you can simmer your stock longer without endangering its flavor or quality.

Stock-Based Soups

The most obvious use of stock is in soups. Even a vegetable soup made with a hearty stock base will taste rich and satisfying.

Sauté onions in butter (or the fat you skimmed from your stock). A lot of caramelization is nice for a beefy stock; merely translucent onions are fine for a chicken or fish soup. Add stock, vegetables, herbs, and salt, bring to a simmer, and cook until tender. Add some finely minced garlic and turn off the heat. Adjust the seasonings once the garlic flavor has infused the soup. You can also add back any of the meat you took from the bones.

—R

Reduction Sauces

Concentrated homemade stocks are *gold.* All that simmering snips proteins into little fragments, in much the same way that fermentation creates magically flavorful miso and tamari from bland soybeans and Parmesan from plain milk. This savory flavor is most apparent when you concentrate your stock by boiling it down. And then the gelatin in the concentrated stock gives it a wonderful lingering, silky texture.

Simple Reduction Gravy

I prefer a simple reduction gravy to flour-thickened gravy, and it's just as easy.

Chop 2 onions and cook them in several tablespoons of butter or fat in a large, heavy skillet until golden brown. Pour in 2 cups or so of homemade stock (not more than halfway up the sides of the skillet, to prevent spatters) and turn the heat way up until it boils madly. Keep a close eye on it for 5 or 10 minutes, until the liquid has mostly boiled off and the onions are starting to brown again. Add another couple of cups of stock, and reduce it again, this time just until it's the consistency of a nice gravy. Add some salt, pepper, and finely minced garlic. Taste and adjust the seasonings.

Depending on the strength of your stock, you might need more than two additions of stock. You could, of course, use a large, tall-sided pot instead of a skillet and add the stock all at once, but it won't be so caramelized.

Serve the gravy very warm, or it will start to gel.

VARIATIONS

The reduction gravy lends itself to adaptation. When you add the stock, include a few tablespoons of wine vinegar or tomato paste (or equivalent quantity of tomato in other forms) to give it some balancing piquancy. Try fresh herbs like thyme, sage, or rosemary, added at the end, or spices like cumin, chili, or cinnamon, added with the stock. Include small bits of meat picked from the stock bones, or chopped giblets. Brown some ground meat along with the onions for a delicious meat sauce.

Reduction Stews

If you have stock near at hand, you can easily create last-minute stews with the flavor of something that spent all afternoon braising.

Brown a chopped onion in butter or fat in a wide, deep pot. Chop celery and carrots fairly small, and cut potatoes or sweet potatoes into larger pieces because they cook more quickly. Add these with 1 quart of stock, 1 to 2 tablespoons of tomato paste, salt, pepper, and any herbs or spices you'd like. Cook it over medium-high heat, stirring occasionally to be sure the vegetables aren't sticking. In 20 minutes, it should be significantly reduced and the potatoes should help thicken it into a good stew consistency. Add some minced garlic, adjust the seasonings, and serve.

Again, this is just a general method. You should vary it according to your fancy and what's on hand.

—R

Stock for Construction: Aspic

Very strong stock will set up like Jell-O when it cools. Nowadays people don't often exploit this amazing property—perhaps it got associated with Jell-O salads and lost favor along with them. But consider the possibilities! Liquid stock mixed into mayonnaise chills into an excellent glaze for cold meats. Warm stock mixed into bits of cooked meat and poured into a greased loaf pan will chill into a delicious, sliceable terrine. The key is to ensure beforehand that your stock is strong enough: Chill it thoroughly and check that it has a nice bouncy-firm consistency (but not rubbery or gummy). If it isn't strong enough, boil it down some more. If it's too strong, dilute it gradually with a little water. You'll also need to skim the fat quite carefully. Season it well, and use it more in a sauce-like supporting role—a filler or glue or layer of glaze—than as a savory version of Jell-O Jigglers.

—R

Chicken Feet

I had a pop-up book when I was young, with terrible witches and misers and mysterious cats popping out all over. The text was a translation of the start of a Pushkin poem, and I can still recite most of it by heart. My favorite page featured the pop-up house of Baba Yaga, with dark pop-up pines leaning in close.

On chicken feet there stands a cottage,
No doors, no windows, bare and lone.
Upon the sands of hidden pathways
Lie tracks of creatures unbeknown.

Unbeknown? Whatever it takes to make it scan in English.

Oh, it was magical. The book didn't go into any more detail about the hut; I had no idea it was a central part of the Baba Yaga lore. It was just a chilling, gratuitous puzzle, and I studied those pop-up feet intently.

This is all to say that chicken feet are witchy. They are also extremely practical, adding lots of velvety density to your chicken stock. But oh! the Quetzalcoatl reptilian skin! the toenails! Such things call for cauldrons, and upon such things my house should stand.

Well, my house does stand on chicken feet. Because my house stands on cookery (as well as books and love), and chicken stock is a firm foundation for my cookery (with a few other things, like good butter), and the stock made from chicken feet is a strong stock, indeed.

Most chicken feet you buy in a store will come from young, tender chickens. They will probably also be clean. If you have just butchered an old hen that doesn't lay anymore or a handsome but superfluous rooster with four-inch spurs on each foot, you will need to work a little harder to get your chicken feet ready for stock making.

Those old roosters grow dragon's hide on their feet, and no amount of scrubbing will ever get them properly clean. It's as if the filth had grown into the scales themselves. Your only recourse is to peel them. Dunk the feet in boiling water for 5 minutes, drain, and clip off the ends of the toes (to remove the toenails). Then get someone to help you painstakingly peel off the outer layer of scaly skin. It will be worth it. Dragon stock is gorgeous. You could walk on it and not fall in.

Wash the feet again and add them to your stock. When the stock is finished and you strain it, don't be shy about sampling the juicy little pads of the feet.

—R

Gizzard and Heart Paprikash

Poultry gizzards and hearts are delicious dark, dark meat—almost blue, they're so dark—but they take a little stewing to become tender. The gizzard is a powerful disc-shaped muscle in the chicken's neck, which grinds seeds and grass. To get the partially digested food out of the gizzard, you have to split it open and peel the lining out, which is why gizzards have that clamshell shape when you buy them.

I first had zúza paprikás, aka gizzard paprikash, one evening in Budapest and later worked up this recipe with help from a laboriously translated page of a Hungarian cookbook. It has a boldly orange, piquant, and creamy sauce.

Back in San Francisco, I wanted to compare my recipe to that in a book I own called *Cooking with Love and Paprika* by Joseph Pasternak (published in 1966). To my alarm, I saw he makes a distinction between Hungarian paprikash and Transylvanian paprikash; according to him, my recipe is Transylvanian because it includes sour cream. How perplexing. Well, the zúza paprikás I had in Hungary most definitely had sour cream in it, just like practically everything I ate there (oh sigh!). Also, a good bit of Transylvania used to belong to Hungary, so maybe it's a moot point.

Many Hungarian dishes start with rendering some minced smoked pork fat in a skillet. Unfortunately, I cannot walk two blocks to the nearest market hall and ask for a kilo of smoked Mangalica fat from the butcher. (Nor can I ask for a kilo of goose gizzards or a quart of pickled peppers ladled from the brine vat or get my jug filled up with raw milk for a handful of forints—sigh, sigh, and sigh.) So I would recommend frying a few slices of bacon at a fairly low temperature for a long time, so the fat renders out without burning at all. Pour the clean fat into a jar, eat the bacon, and clean the sticky stuff off the skillet before putting the fat back in. This will give you good fat with a nice smoky flavor.

You may chop the gizzards or hearts before cooking them; when cooked, a whole gizzard tends to be a bit more than one mouthful. You can also remove the "hinge" in the middle of the gizzard—this is the most sinewy part—and then the gizzards will become tender much sooner. I lazily leave my gizzards whole.

Mince a large onion fairly fine, and let it cook in the fat in a Dutch oven till soft and clear. Push the onions to one side of the Dutch oven and briefly brown about 1 pound of gizzards and/or hearts on the other side.

Add salt and a large peeled, crushed tomato (or a tablespoon of paste), and a ton of fresh sweet paprika, 2 to 3 tablespoons.* Pour in enough chicken stock to cover the gizzards, cover the pan, and let it simmer for about 3 hours, until the meat is tender. Undercooked gizzards are unpleasantly squeaky on the tooth. If you trimmed the gizzards, they may only take an hour or so to cook.

If the dish seems too liquid (soupy, not stewy), remove the lid and let it boil down for a bit. When it's done cooking, add a couple of cloves of finely minced garlic and turn off the heat. Swirl in sour cream or crème fraîche to taste—at least ½ cup. Taste and adjust the seasonings. Paprikash is traditionally served over little egg noodles (tojásos tészta). Any fresh pasta will work fine, and I sometimes eat it on potatoes.

You can also use this recipe to make straight-up chicken paprikash. Break a small young chicken down into drumsticks, thighs, wings, and breasts. It will only need 45 minutes or so of cooking time, and you can let the chicken pieces make their own stock as they cook. Add the breasts toward the end of the cooking time so they don't get overdone. Old stewing birds will take about 3 hours, just like the gizzards.

*About the paprika: It really needs to be of good quality if you're using it for more than simply sprinkling on deviled eggs. *Fresh* means less than a year old. *Sweet* means it's made from sweet peppers, not spicy ones. It's hard to find nonsweet paprika in the United States, so you probably don't need to worry about it.

—R

Marrow Bones

Quite simple to prepare and primally satisfying, marrow bones are one of my all-time favorite treats. If you want them fancier, soak them in several changes of salted water in the refrigerator for a day to draw out the blood. The blood, however, is no disaster if you need your marrow bones right away.

Place the bone chunks on end in a skillet or rimmed baking sheet and roast for 15 minutes at 425°F. Bone sections more than a few inches high may take 5 minutes longer. The marrow swells up as it heats. Don't overbake it or the marrow will just melt and run off.

Serve hot with crackers or toast, salt, pepper, and little spoons or knives for digging out the marrow.

—R

Pork and Sauerkraut

Pork with sauerkraut is an effortless slow-braised transmutation. The acidic sauerkraut makes the pork tender, cuts its richness, and cooks down into a pungent golden mess. The aroma—even the thought of it—also happens to make my eyes well up with homesickness.

Choose a couple of pounds of bone-in pork roast, ribs, or other cheap cut of pork. The bones contribute so much flavor to the sauerkraut juices—don't neglect them.

Heat a few tablespoons of fat in the bottom of a Dutch oven. When it's shimmery and hot, add the meat in a single layer on the bottom. Turn it after 1 or 2 minutes to brown it on the other side.

When the meat is well browned, add 1 quart of sauerkraut and its juices. If the kraut is fairly dry, you'll want to add some liquid to keep it from burning. Stir it a bit to loosen any meat bits stuck to the bottom of the pot. Consider adding ½ cup of applesauce or a fresh apple, peeled, cored, and chunked to sweeten the sauce. A few halved onions are also delicious, but the critical thing here is the kraut.

Cover the pot and let it cook gently for 5 hours or more, checking occasionally to make sure the liquid doesn't cook off. The pork will be falling apart when it's done, and the sauerkraut will reduce and soften.

Serve the pork on mashed potatoes, topped with the cooked-down sauerkraut.

—R

4
Fish

When we think of our rapidly depleting commercial fishing stocks, compounded with utterly flavorless farmed fish that are now becoming ubiquitous, what can we suggest but grabbing a rod and reel, a little hillock to contemplate existence, and finding the leisure to join the noble ranks of famed anglers like Sir Isaak Walton? Nor should we neglect the small fry, the lovely little oily sprat and herring. And what has become of the unctuous carcasses that one so rarely sees still connected to fish filets? Here are a few ideas intended to restore our appreciation for fish beyond the bland overfished standards.

Smoked Trout

If you can get your hands on fresh brook trout, or actually any species, this is an exquisite way to serve it. The first time I tasted smoked trout was at the high table at Trinity College Oxford where I spent a summer ages ago. Neither person on either side of me liked it, so I ate three portions and nothing else! All you need is a regular small kettle barbecue grill and a bag of wood chips soaked in good ruddy red wine. Mesquite is good but very strong, hickory a little less intense, and apple and cherry are delightful.

First you must use the whole fish—skin, head, and all. Only the guts should be removed. Salt the trout well and set aside for several hours or overnight in the fridge. This not only flavors but firms up the flesh. When ready, pat the fish dry and put some fresh herbs like dill or tarragon into the cavity. Start a small fire with some real hardwood charcoal (not briquettes). You need only a couple of handfuls. When charcoal begins to glow, throw on your wood chips, set the grate in place, put the fish on, and cover the whole thing. The grill will smoke like mad. After 15 or 20 minutes, remove the fish. Don't overcook them. They should be just barely cooked through. You can eat them hot, the skin peels back easily and the meat comes right off the bones, or save them for later and eat chilled. In the latter case, a little crème fraîche with dill is lovely. This is technically a hot-smoke method, but trout can also be cold smoked (see page 66). Other whole fish can also be used if you don't have trout, as long as the flesh is firm enough so it doesn't fall apart.

Another great trick with trout comes from one of my favorite authors, physician and polymath Girolamo Cardano, who lived in sixteenth-century Italy. He wrote a horoscope for the young future king Edward VI of England, predicting a long and happy reign. Well, he muffed that one. This recipe made its way into a compendium of alchemy and household hints by Jacob Wecker (whose wife wrote a great cookbook, by the way) and this in turn was translated into English as *Secrets of Art and Nature* in 1661. It's a bizarre book, including things like how "to rost a Goose alive," which "will be almost eaten up before he be dead, it is very pleasant to behold." I think not. But the following recipe is excellent:

> *How to fry Fish upon a Paper as well as with a Frying-Pan. Take a single Paper and raising up the sides like to a Lamp, pour in Oyl, and before it soak through, set it upon the clear coles without any flame, for the Oyl will not pass through, avoiding the fire, nor will the Paper burn because it cannot dry, the Oyl preserving it. But fire cannot be without extream dryness, nor can flame or motion so attenuate as to make it burn, but it will grow hot by degrees putting under fresh coals, and so it will boyl, which is very strange, for the fishes will be well fryed in it.*

The next time you are out camping or fishing, just whip out a piece of parchment paper and give this a shot. It does work. The paper should be set directly on the coals, not on the grate if you do this in a barbecue grill. In the latter case, I would suggest you try fresh sardines, which are always nice when they come near hot coals.

—K

Tonno Sott'Olio

If you want to replicate canned tuna, you will need a pressure canner, special equipment, and a good insurance policy. I don't know how it's done, honestly, but tonno sott'olio is far more interesting. Start with a really fresh sushi-grade tuna, cut into 2- or 3-inch batons. Season them with salt, tarragon, or dill and let marinate a few hours. Follow the directions for hot smoking on page 80, but instead of eating the tuna, put the pieces in a jar, cover in olive oil, and seal tightly. Let the tuna rest several weeks in a cool dark place. They don't have to be in the fridge, but you can store the jar there if you like. It will make the oil opaque though. When you open the jar, remove the fish from the oil, and serve on toast or crusty bread. The oil is also delicious, so don't throw it away.

You can also keep baby artichokes this way. Trim off the outer leaves, cut in half, and remove the fuzzy choke in the middle. Peel the stem, too, and immediately sprinkle with lemon juice so they don't brown. Next blanch the artichokes in boiling water for about 5 minutes. Salt them well, drizzle on some olive oil, and more lemon. Then put them on the barbecue and grill. Don't smoke them, but cook through, full throttle as you would any other food. When lightly charred, if you can resist popping them into your mouth immediately, plunge them into oil in a jar, cover, and let the flavors combine for a few weeks. These are just delectable. Large artichokes can be cooked the same way, blanched a little bit longer, and grilled longer as well, but they don't do as well in the oil.

—K

Garum

The ancient Romans were crazy about a fish sauce called garum or liquamen. There were many different versions, some thick and more like a paste, some thin and probably not too different from the Southeast Asian fish sauce nuoc mam or nam pla. The Romans used it in practically every savory dish, and combined with honey, pepper, and vinegar the sauce is truly exquisite. It is said to survive in southern Italy in the form of colatura, but in fact this is just liquid drained off of salted gutted and headless anchovies. Good, but not really garum.

There is still great debate over what garum was exactly, especially which fish should be used. Gargilius Martialis has a fairly quick recipe that uses sardines. The *Geoponica* mentions smelts or sprat or mackerel or a combination of these. There is also a version made with tuna guts and blood. Naturally I wanted the version that takes longest. Here's how: Find 1 pound or however much you want, of small fish, like smelts or fresh anchovies. Don't gut them, it's the intestines that create the ferment. Salt them really well and put into a ceramic jar, covered. Put this in the sun for 3 months. Contrary to what most people think, they don't smell at all. They smell fishy when fresh, but after they start fermenting, the aroma becomes sweet. Strain them very carefully, not pressing on the solids, and you have some dark brown, lovely salty garum.

The following recipe comes from the great cookbook author Apicius, compiled around the fourth century CE. Well, at least it's attributed to him—a great gourmand who, when he found his money dwindling and realized he could no longer dine in grand style, poisoned himself. Trust me, it wasn't the garum! It is one of my favorites, such a riot of flavors and textures.

Apricot Minutal

In a pan put oil, garum, wine, chopped dried shallots, and cubed cooked pork shoulder. This being cooked, pound pepper, cumin, dried mint and dill, soak with honey, garum, raisin wine, a bit of vinegar, some of the cooking broth, and then temper. Add Pitted apricots and let them cook through. Crumble in tracta to thicken, sprinkle with pepper and serve.

To *temper* just means to gently mix together. The *tracta* were thin sheets of baked dough, sort of like a cracker, used to thicken dishes. Use some broken-up crackers.

—K

Fish Head Stew

I should tell you that I saw the ocean only once before I was sixteen. Until then, my notion of seafood consisted of plastic trays of shrimp at buffet receptions, sunfish caught in our pond, tinned sardines, and the occasional snapping turtle that wandered up into the yard. That, and Christmas Eve oyster stew.

Then I landed in the West Coast and promptly fell to slurping oysters out of their shells, cracking crab legs, and pestering fishmongers. I started to think I was ocean savvy.

One day I got a salmon head at market, lured by its shockingly low price. It was nothing short of a revelation. It brought me to my knees and left me giddy. It was like I'd been eating chicken breast for years and only just discovered chickens had drumsticks. Like I'd been eating pork chops but never had *bacon*.

The meat on salmon heads is identifiably salmon, but richer, creamier, shiveringly succulent. And quite unlike salmon fillets, a stewed salmon head can fill up two people for less than $5. Provided, of course, that you eat the eyeballs. Just spit out that little white ball bearing thing in the middle.

You can use other large fish heads in this recipe. But nice oily fish will be the most rewarding.

Stewing a fish head is almost exactly like making stock with it: Cover it with water and bring it to a gentle, gentle simmer for 30 minutes. Delicate fish bones readily render up their flavor and gelatin in that amount of time. Much longer, and the oils will oxidize and taste terrible.

Instead of simply straining out the head, as you might with small fish, and proceeding to make soup with the stock, you want to spend 10 minutes laboriously picking all the fish meat off the head. Don't be shy of the skin; near the head, the skin is thick and tender. Pull out the bones where you can, but some will inevitably slip through. Above all, cherish the cheeks! Those boneless little morsels are such a treasure. And I wasn't kidding about the eyes. They might scare your guests, though, so be sure to eat them all yourself.

Before you return the saved meat to the broth, you'll want to season it. Some ideas: ginger, miso, and noodles or a bit of tomato, garlic, and dill or just salt, pepper, and lemon. Add the fish back to the broth after the heat is off, to avoid overcooking it.

—R

Cured Fish

The refrigerator has extended the shelf life of most things we buy, with the exception of fresh fish—which must be kept on ice just as it was a hundred years ago, and even then doesn't keep more than a day or two. Unless you live next door to a fishmonger, that means fish is the fussy part of your dinner plans. It doesn't have to be.

Salt is the ancient refrigerator. It's a remarkably convenient one, even for the modern kitchen. Not only does it preserve delicate flesh like fish but it transforms it into a new delicacy, too—firming up the flesh and mellowing the flavor.

This method works exceptionally well for inexpensive small, oily fish—like sardines—or larger oily fish—like herring. The nomenclature is actually quite ambiguous because *sardine* refers to many different species of silvery small, oily fish. *Herring* refers to closely related slightly larger oily fish, which in some cases are simply grown-up sardines. I use sardines, because they're plentiful here in San Francisco. You can also salt down fillets of large fish, like cod.

Small fish usually come whole, not gutted. To clean them, rub them down to remove any clinging scales, slice off their heads just behind the gills, and slit their bellies down to the vent. Scoop out the loose guts and rinse the fish off. I like to perform the whole operation in the sink.

These fish are very delicate and break down quickly. If you find any fish that are mushy or mealy, feed them to the cat; the salt cure won't fix them.

For each pound of whole fish, allow about ¼ cup of sea salt.

Lay the fish in a single layer in a baking dish. Salt them all over on one side, turn them, and salt them all over on the other side. For small fish, you don't need to try salting them inside. If the whole fish is more than an inch thick, you should sprinkle salt in the cavity, too.

The fish will exude liquid as the salt contracts their flesh. You could set the fish on a rack inside the pan, or just remember to pour out the liquid twice a day while they cure.

Cover the dish securely and refrigerate.

You can try your fish after 24 hours of curing. As the cure progresses, the muscles will shrink up and release from the bones. If the cure goes too long, the fish will simply dry onto the bone and become rather jerky-like. I find 48 hours of curing is about perfect for small fish.

Open up the cured fish and gently loosen the spine. The larger bones should unzip along with it, and a sharp tug at the end will pop off the tail, too. Peel the fillets out from the skin. Try one! The texture will be like lox or gravlax. If they cured for a long time and are very salty, you will need to soak them in cool water for a several hours or up to a day, changing the water.

Fish cured like this will keep for a week or two in the fridge. If you want to make something that can keep longer (salt cod, say), you'll need to use more salt—enough to really bury the fish. Then cure it for a full week (whole fish should be boned partway through the week).

Then you can make your own salt cod brandade, with the recipe found in *The Lost Art of Real Cooking.*

Or you can pickle your fish.

—R

Pickled Fish

A very traditional treatment for herring that works quite well with sardines, too, is to pickle the fish. First, salt-cure the fish for 24 to 48 hours. If you started with about 2 pounds of small whole fish, this recipe will fit perfectly in a quart jar. If you're using large fillets, your yield may be a little greater and you'll need to cut the cured fillets down into 1-inch pieces.

Layer the fish in a quart jar with a small thinly sliced onion and a few bay leaves. For aesthetic purposes, you can stack the fillets with the jar on its side, so they're packed in vertically when you turn it upright. This also makes it easier to nab a single fillet with your fork when it's snack time later.

Mix together 1 cup of strong vinegar and ¼ cup of sugar. White vinegar is fine here or apple cider or wine vinegar—but nothing with weird additives or overwhelming flavors. If you're using homemade vinegar, be sure it's quite strong or it won't sufficiently pickle the fish.

Pour the vinegar mixture over the fish in the jar. Top off with more vinegar to cover the fish and onions completely. Screw on the lid and refrigerate for at least 3 or 4 days before you sample the fish.

Feel free to play around with the brine. Try white wine vinegar with honey instead of sugar, and several tablespoons of mustard thrown in. Pack in a few sprigs of fresh dill or other herbs.

—R

5

Dairy and Eggs

Abundant in certain seasons and sparse in others, milk and eggs have found themselves preserved and transformed over the years into some of the strangest delicacies. In this chapter we have collected a few of the most remarkable dairy and egg recipes for your experimentation. We subject milk and eggs to mold, caramelization, pickling, and vigorous boiling—from simple fresh cheeses like paneer and chèvre to thousand-year-old eggs and Camembert. Plus we include a recipe for ambergris, which we put in a chapter on milk and eggs because it also comes from a living animal—a whale.

Cheeses

Paneer

The absolute easiest cheese to make and one that really captures the fresh flavor of milk is Indian paneer. It is like the gateway drug for addict cheese makers. Use regular whole milk, and the only equipment you need is a pot, a colander, some cheesecloth, and string. Bring 1 gallon of milk almost to the boiling point and stir continuously. Then pour in the juice of 2 lemons. Some people use vinegar, but the flavor of the lemons works so nicely. Keep stirring and you will see the whole mass curdle, at which point turn off the heat and let this sit for a few minutes. Then line a sieve or colander with the cheesecloth, put it over a big bowl or pot and gently pour in the whole pot of curds and whey. Save the whey for another use. Let the curds drain for about 1 hour, wrapped in the cheesecloth, tied at the top with string. Then put the curds, still wrapped in cheesecloth, under a board and weigh them down for a few hours or more with a heavy object on top. The cheese is traditionally cut into cubes and cooked in dishes like saag paneer with spinach and spices. Finely chop the spinach and cook slowly with a little water and onions, turmeric, fenugreek, cumin, and the like. Just delicious.

If you care to experiment, before the draining is done, add a few pinches of salt and mix well, then continue with the draining and pressing. Most paneer is not salted this way, but it will allow you to keep it longer. It will come out a little drier and firmer than most paneer. At this point I like to cut the cheese into cubes, put the cubes in a jar, and cover with olive oil that's been flavored with herbs. The cheese bites are amazing as a snack or used in cooked dishes. I really don't know how long these will last because I've never been able to keep the cheese around for very long, but they should be fine for a few weeks in a cool place. They can also be used in any recipe that calls for feta or even on a pizza, though they won't melt. The taste is phenomenal.

—K

Mozzarella

People seem to love the stringy rubbery low-moisture mozzarella that dominates the market. You can find soft delicate fresh little bocconcini and larger balls, too, but it is so much fun to make and tastes so much more like fresh milk that you must try it. Start with really good milk, preferably organic, and preferably raw. You can use ordinary milk, but then you get ordinary cheese. Here it really does make a huge difference because you'll be eating this absolutely fresh and young. Suckling baby cheese.

The basic procedure is the same as for aged harder cheeses, and you can find a full explanation in our last book. I'll run you through the process very quickly here. Heat 2 gallons of milk on the stovetop to 90°F and turn off the heat. You don't need a culture here because this is fresh cheese, so put 20 drops of liquid rennet in a bowl with 1 cup of water, and stir this into the milk. Some people add citric acid at this point, too, which makes it stringier and firmer, but I prefer a softer cheese. Let this sit for 45 to 60 minutes, monitoring the temperature with a thermometer and turning on the heat if necessary to maintain 90°F, but not disturbing the formation of the curd in any way. When it turns into a solid jellied mass, cut the curds gently with a knife in a checkerboard pattern. Let them sit over heat for 20 to 30 minutes to let the whey seep from the curds. Turn up the heat and let the curds rise to about 98°F and leave the pot for about 30 minutes more. Turn off the heat once you've reached 98°F. The curds will become heavy and sink. With your hands remove the curds and put them into a bowl. Or you can also just carefully pour off the whey and leave the curds in the pot. They will continue to exude whey; keep pouring it off. Salt the curds a little, but don't break them up.

Pour the whey through a strainer to remove the last of any curds, and return the whey to the pot. Now boil the whey vigorously and skim off any solids that rise to the top. This is ricotta, the real thing.

Next is the really tricky and fun part, forming the mozzarella. Take a ladle of your really hot whey and pour it over the curds (160°F is hot enough). Put your hand right into it and start massaging the cheese. You can either use a stick, so you don't burn your hands, or have a bowl of ice water nearby and keep your hands chilled. What you're doing is kneading the curds into a semimelted mass. Keep adding super-hot whey and keep folding the curds over and pressing down on them; the folding is what makes the final product stringy, in Italian a *pasta filata.* Now squeeze off balls of the cheese and put into a container and cover with the whey, very well salted. You'll see that the whey becomes milky and has drawn some of the fat off the cheese. These, incidentally, can be tiny bocconcini (little mouthfuls) or tennis ball–size pieces. Put the mozzarella in its liquid into the fridge and let cool. It is best to leave it a little while lest the cheese be "squeaky" on your teeth. But if you can't wait, that's fine. If you really want squeaky cheese, don't put it in liquid and use it up in a few days.

You can cook with this cheese, though it won't melt quite

like low-moisture mozzarella we get in this country. It can go on a pizza, too, but should just be thinly sliced and laid on a thin crust, cooked at no less than 800°F, preferably in a wood-burning oven. In lieu of that, just make a good insalata caprese, with the best tomatoes, leaves of basil, and with slices of this mozzarella. Add a drizzle of olive oil, a touch of sea salt, and be transported.

—K

Chèvre

You can make delicious fresh goat cheese in one of two ways. The quickest way uses rennet, and the slow method is basically a strained yogurt cheese. The rennet makes a grainier cheese, while the slow method makes a glossy smooth chèvre. In both cases you must be sure to get goat's milk that is not ultra-pasteurized. Sadly, most of the leading brands of goat milk are ultra-pasteurized and are too cooked to make a good cheese. Check at farmers' markets and ask at health food stores. Local cheese makers should also know of a good source for fresh goat's milk.

For the quick method—which still takes several hours—gently heat 1 gallon of fresh goat's milk up to 85° to 90°F. Mix a little of the warm milk with ¼ teaspoon of mesophilic cheese culture or 1 tablespoon of fresh yogurt, and stir well. Turn off the heat and cover the pot for 1 hour.

Gently bring the pot back up to 85° to 90°F. Mix ⅛ teaspoon of rennet with 2 tablespoons of cool filtered water. Drizzle over the warm milk and stir well. Turn off the heat, cover, and let sit for 1 hour.

Check that the curds are firm enough to give a clean break

when sliced with a sharp knife. If they're too soft, let the curd keep sitting for another 30 to 60 minutes. When they're ready, cut them into a ½-inch grid with a long, sharp knife, then stir the curds and break them up into ½-inch cubes. Cover the pot and let the curds rest for 15 minutes.

Place a large colander in a large pot and line it with fine-mesh cheesecloth. Ladle the curds into the cheesecloth, tie it up, and hang the curd bag from a wooden spoon or the faucet, with the pot underneath to catch the whey. Poking and shifting the bag can help the whey drain out more quickly.

Let the curds drain until the cheese is the desired consistency. Empty the drained curds into a bowl. Season with 1 teaspoon of salt and serve. Fresh chèvre will keep for a week or more in the fridge, but it's mildest the day it's made. You can also add minced garlic and herbs, or whatever delicious thing you want to fancy it up with.

For a very firm cheese, drain the curds for 1 hour, then mix them with 1 teaspoon of salt and ladle them into a cheese mold—a plastic container with holes poked in the sides and bottom. Set the cheeses in a tray to catch the whey, and let them rest for 2 days. They will shrink down significantly.

For the slower method, gently bring the milk up to 86°F. Mix 1 tablespoon of yogurt culture with the warm milk and stir it in. Mix 2 drops of rennet into 1 tablespoon of cool filtered water, and stir into the milk. Cover the pot with a towel and let it sit overnight.

In the morning, slice the curds inside the pot in a ½-inch grid pattern, making sure the knife goes all the way to the bottom of the pot. Then make more slices at an angle to the surface of the curd, again ½-inch apart. Gently stir the curds, using the spoon to break up any that are significantly larger than ½-inch cubes. Spoon the curds into a cheesecloth-lined colander and drain as described above. Salt to taste and beat the curds with a whisk to make them glossy. This stuff is exquisite with a bit of bold-flavored honey mixed in.

—R

Mysost or Brunost

Mysost cheese is more like a kind of fudge made from whey and goes by various names in Norway and Sweden. The variety likely to be found in the United States is gjetost (goat cheese), a brown caramelized block, best shaved thinly and served on bread. It's quite addictive and simple to make, but will take Herculean patience. After you've made cheese, save the whey, from cow's milk or goat—at least 1 quart. Make sure it's not salted to start, or it will be unpalatable by the end of the process. All you basically do is put the whey in a pot at the lowest possible temperature and let it barely simmer. After 5 or 6 hours it will have reduced almost entirely and will start to get thick and turn light brown—in Norwegian it's called prim at this stage and can be served proper, spread on bread. Or add a few tablespoons of cream and a tiny bit of salt and keep going. Eventually it will look exactly like caramel; watch it carefully to make sure it doesn't burn, stirring from time to time. Finally, you will have a solid brown glob. Scrape it out onto a wooden board and let cool. Then either press it into a square mold or form into a shape that will be easy to slice with a cheese plane. Aesthetically, it is precisely midway between candy and cheese.

—K

Bloomy-Rind Cheese

The bloomy-rind cheeses are those with a layer of mold growing over the outside—the most famous examples being Brie and Camembert. The digestive enzymes in the mold break down the cheese curd, creating a creamy soft cheese inside an aromatic fungal rind. In the United States, you are not allowed to buy such cheeses made from raw milk because they age for less than 60 days and the government wants to protect you from your recklessness.

In other places, people do not have such caring governments, and they eat raw milk Camembert with wild abandon. In fact, the original Camembert, Camembert de Normandie, is a French AOC-protected designation, and the law specifies that it must be made with *only* raw milk. Such cheeses must be enjoyed abroad, as they cannot even be imported into the United States.

If you have a trusted source of good raw milk, however, you can experience the wild thrills of raw milk Camembert in the comfort of your own home. Just be sensible about cleanliness and don't try to sell it to anybody, or you might find yourself face down on the kitchen floor while a heavily armed SWAT team rifles through your cupboards. (Am I exaggerating? No. Milk is a highly controlled substance, and the government is very concerned that you buy only government-approved cheese.)

This recipe works quite well with good pasteurized milk, too. Just be sure it is freshly pasteurized, because there's nothing pure about pasteurized milk that's been handled carelessly and reinfected with harmful bacteria.

The main thing is, with either raw or pasteurized milk, bloomy-rind cheese is a brilliantly *fun* project. Not only can you grow magical gardens of mold and bacteria, but you can even watch your guests' jaws drop in amazement (and hunger) as you place a melting sliver of Camembert on their plates and tell them you made it yourself. It doesn't even require much in the way of special equipment: a small tub or box, some reed mats, a few yogurt containers or tin cans, and some mail-order spores.

These cheeses *are* picky about their environment. Mold cannot thrive in dry air. Luckily, the bloomy-rind molds do quite well at cool temperatures, and this cheese can age in your refrigerator, with some accommodations.

Brie and Camembert are made very similarly, but the large wheel shape commonly used for Brie is more unwieldy for home production. If you like, however, you can follow the same recipe, but shape the cheese in one plate-size circular mold.

You can find your cheese cultures easily online. Get a packet of either Flora Danica or Mesophilic Type B cheese culture. You'll also need a packet of *Penicillium camemberti* mold spores (also called *P. candidum*) and a bottle of rennet. Store the cultures in your freezer until you're ready to use them, and keep the rennet refrigerated. Find a lidded box or plastic tub at least 8 by 12 by 4 inches, and get three small reed mats. The reed mats sold for rolling sushi will work perfectly. Cut or fold one of the mats to fit neatly on the bottom of your plastic tub. Also, get a piece of fine-mesh cheesecloth, about 1 yard square. Most cheesecloth in stores has a very large open weave. You could use this kind if you layer it several times. A fine tea towel, pillowcase, or large napkin would also work well.

You'll then need to make a pair of cheese molds. Look for a cylindrical plastic jug, quart-size yogurt container, or aluminum can—something about 5 inches in diameter and 6 inches tall, with straightish sides (if the sides are slightly angled, your cheese will just be somewhat less perfect looking). Cut the bottom out of the mold so it's open on both ends, and trim it so the cut edge is smooth and level. Then poke large holes in the sides of the container with a clean nail or other sharp device, every inch or so. Poke the holes from the inside out, so the interior of the mold stays smooth.

In the morning of your cheese-making day, heat 1 gallon of good fresh whole milk (raw or pasteurized; avoid ultra-pasteurized) and 1 pint of cream over a very low flame. Stir it frequently until it comes to 86°F. Turn off the heat (if you have an electric stove, you will need to move the pot off the burner) and sprinkle over the milk ¼ teaspoon of cheese culture (the Flora Danica or Mesophilic Type B) and ⅛ teaspoon of *P. camemberti* mold culture. Stir gently, cover the pot, and drape a towel over

A quart-sized store-bought yogurt container makes a serviceable cheese mold.

top. Leave the thermometer in the pot so you can keep an eye on the temperature.

After 90 minutes of culturing, check the temperature. Turn the heat on for just a moment while stirring the milk, until it's up to 90°F. Dilute ⅛ teaspoon of rennet in 2 tablespoons of cool filtered water. Drizzle it into the milk and stir gently for 1 minute. Cover the pot again and leave it undisturbed for 90 minutes.

While the cheese is setting up, heat a large pot of water up to boiling. Submerge your cheesecloth, molds, cheese mats, and two cutting boards, and set aside to drip dry somewhere very clean.

When 90 minutes have passed, the milk should have firmed up into a nice curd. Insert a long knife into the curd and pull it out. There should be a clean edge to the hole the knife left behind, indicating a firm curd. If it's a little more pudding-like, leave the curd for another 30 minutes or more.

If the curds are firm, slice them inside the pot in a ½-inch grid pattern, making sure the knife goes all the way to the bottom of the pot. Then make more slices at an angle to the surface of the curd, again ½-inch apart. Gently stir the curds, using a spoon to break up any that are significantly larger than ½-inch cubes—but avoid mashing the curds. Stirring gently, turn the heat on once more and carefully bring the temperature back up to 90°F. Turn off the heat, cover the pot, and let the curds rest for 15 minutes.

After the 15-minute rest, the curds will have contracted and firmed up a bit. Place a colander in a bowl and line it with the cheesecloth. Ladle the curds into the cheesecloth and tie the corners together. If your sink is deep enough, you can hang the curds from the faucet, but a large wooden spoon placed on the backs of two chairs makes a good rack, too. Leave the bowl under the suspended bag of curds to catch the dripping whey.

Let the whey drain for about 30 minutes. Shift and tug the bag around to keep the whey draining freely. Meanwhile, you can set up your cheese molds. Place one of the cutting boards in a tray to catch the whey runoff, and put a reed mat on top of the board. If your cheese molds are not perfect cylinders, set them on the reed mat with the narrow end down.

Ladle the drained curds into the two prepared cheese molds. The curds should not fill the molds all the way to the top. Cover the molds with another reed mat and the other cutting board. Let them drain for 3 to 4 hours. As the whey seeps out under the gentle weight of the curds, the cheeses will shrink down and firm up.

When the cheeses hold their shape, you can flip them. Lift the cutting-board-cheese-mold stack out of the tray and carefully flip it over. Set the stack down and take a peek at your cheeses: They should have released from the reed mats and dropped down in the molds. If they haven't, you can peel the mat back by curling it away from the cheese to loosen it up.

Flip the cheese several times more during the next 12 to 18 hours. They should stay out at room temperature on your counter. When the cheeses are just a couple of inches high or so and fairly sturdy, they're ready to salt down and cure.

Now it's time to prepare the curing chamber! Sterilize your curing box or tub in boiling water, along with the third mat you cut to fit inside of it. When they're cool, place the mat in the box. Find a relatively warm corner of your refrigerator for the box to live for the next 2 months; 45°F is ideal. Check with a thermometer: it's surprising how much temperature variation there is be-

tween the back and front and top and bottom of a refrigerator. If it's a little too cold, that's fine; the cheese will just take longer to ripen.

Sprinkle ½ teaspoon of very fine sea salt evenly on each surface of the cheese—that's 1½ teaspoons per cheese. Salt on the exterior of the cheese protects it from opportunistic foreign mold during the early weeks of ripening. By the end of the ripening period, the saltiness will be evenly distributed throughout the cheese.

Place the salted cheeses on the reed mat in the box, with room for air to circulate around them. Put the lid on securely and put the whole thing in its special mold-friendly ripening spot in the fridge.

During the next few days, keep an eye on the box to fine-tune the cheeses' environment. You want it to be quite humid, so condensation on the inside of the box is to be expected. If there's no condensation, pour a few tablespoons of cool sterile water onto the reed mat. Keep a thermometer in the box to make sure the temperature is staying where you want it. I find that I need to turn the box regularly because one end always gets cooler than the other.

After a week or so, the mold will start to grow. It starts as spots of fluffy snow-white fuzz and eventually grows to cover the entire surface. If the mold takes longer to form—two weeks, say—then you know your box has been too cold. Apart from slowing down the cheese's progress, the cold is not a terrible problem; however, you'll want to remember that the cheese is a late bloomer when you come to the later stages of ripening.

When there's a nice solid blanket of mold, turn the cheeses over. You will have to carefully peel them off the mat; curl it back reed-by-reed to release the cheese. Keep turning the cheese every few days to prevent the mold from permanently fusing the cheese to the mat.

Once I had to leave town at this point in the ripening process, and when I returned, the mold had started eating the mat, turning the reeds punky and swallowing them into the cheese. The cheese was fine with a little trimming, but the mat was not.

Though it probably won't be an issue if you sterilized your equipment and salted the cheese thoroughly, keep a sharp eye out for dark mold of any sort. If you see any, cut it out immediately and dab vinegar over the incision site.

When the cheese is thoroughly coated with a thick blanket of white mold (after another week or so), you can wrap it. You could also just leave it as is, but the wrapping saves you from having to flip it. If you buy specialty cheese paper, you can even get rid of the ripening box entirely at this point, since the cheese paper holds in enough humidity while allowing the cheese to breathe. However, you will do just fine by wrapping the cheeses in parchment and leaving them in the box. In any case, keep the cheeses at the same warm-refrigerator temperature.

Now comes the hardest part: knowing when to cut into the

cheese. Once you sample it, the ripening process comes to a halt. Of course, even a slightly underripe cheese is still delicious; the edges will be creamy even if the center is a bit firm and chalky (and this is exactly how some cheeses are supposed to be eaten). At the very least, though, wait 4 weeks after wrapping the cheese, and then start looking for ripeness cues.

A ripe cheese has a firm rind with a soft interior. It will give in the middle when gently pressed, even if the rind feels stiff. The surface of the cheese will become a bit swaybacked, sagging slightly from the edge.

You might even insert a very sharp, narrow, sterile knife into the middle of the cheese to feel if there is a firm resistance—if there is, pull that knife out and wrap that cheese back up. If you're lucky, the mold will grow back over the cut and nobody will know. Try again in another few weeks.

If your mold took a long time to form in the early stages of ripening, you will want to allow extra ripening time now. Two months from the wrapping date.

And if you neglect your cheese? If its environment got too warm, and it ripened up while you weren't paying attention? Overripe cheese easily develops an acrid cat-pee ammonia aroma. The center of the cheese may still be okay, however, as the ripening proceeds from the outside in.

Bloomy-rind cheeses are best shown off and served at room temperature. Let them warm up on the counter for ½ hour or so before eating. Once cut, keep them wrapped in parchment in a loose plastic bag in the fridge.

—R

Feta

A deliciously tangy pickled cheese, feta is also very beautiful, but we don't often get the chance to see. Usually it's obscured by a plastic container with a little brine sloshing around. When you make it at home, you can put it in a pretty glass jar and admire it every time you open the fridge.

Feta is often made with sheep's milk or some combination of goat's, sheep's, and cow's milk. Unfortunately, sheep's milk can be difficult to source, but you can make feta with just goat's or cow's milk, too. Be careful: More obscure milks like goat's are often only available ultra-pasteurized, which does not work for cheese. My sister-in-law, Carrie Nafziger Figueroa, sent me a recipe, which I have adapted here.

Put 1 gallon of whole milk, raw or pasteurized, in a large pot. Bring it up to 90°F and turn off the heat. Blend 1 tablespoon of fresh, live-culture yogurt with a few tablespoons of the warm milk and stir into the pot. You can also use ¼ teaspoon cheese culture (Flora Danica left over from making Camembert, say).

Stir ⅛ teaspoon of rennet into 2 tablespoons of cool, filtered water. Add to the milk pot and stir gently. Cover the pot and let it sit for a few hours or overnight.

In the morning, bring the temperature gently up to 90°F, turn off the heat, and cut the curd into ½-inch cubes, as described for Camembert. Stir gently and let the curds sit for 15 minutes to contract. Ladle the curds into a large colander lined with fine cheesecloth and set over a pot or bowl. Tie up the corners of the cheesecloth and hang it over the pot to collect the draining whey. Because you'll make the pickling brine from the whey, it's extra important that you save it carefully.

Let the curds drain for about 6 hours. You want them to hold their shape well, but not be dried out. Empty the curds into a bowl and toss with ½ teaspoon fine sea salt.

Make a small cheese mold by poking large holes in a 2-pound can or quart-size yogurt container. Line the mold with a layer of fine cheesecloth, undyed cloth napkin, or multiple layers of coarse cheesecloth, and scoop the curds into the mold. Wrap the cheesecloth over the top of the cheese and find an object that fits inside of the mold that can act as a weight—a mason jar, for example, or a smaller can or plastic container, or the lid of the can with a weight on top. Stack a cutting board or mortar or other heavy objects on top—you want about 5 pounds of pressure just to squeeze out a little more whey.

Let the cheese sit under the weight for 24 hours. You want it to be quite firm and hold its shape well, or else it will just dissolve into the brine when you pickle it.

Find a wide-mouth quart jar to use for brining the cheese. Cut the cheese into chunks that will fit in the jar—2- to 3-inch cubes are about right. Mix 2½ cups of saved whey with 5 tablespoons of fine sea salt. Place the cheese chunks in the jar and pour the brine over top so it covers the cheese. Refrigerate.

You can try the feta after 4 or 5 days of pickling, but it will continue to ripen for a month or so. It keeps for a couple of months. This brining method makes a very salty, pickled cheese. If the cheese is too salty for your taste, you can rinse it in cool water before using it. I like it as is, particularly crumbled over a salad.

This recipe scales nicely if you have a large enough pickling vessel and space in your refrigerator. The brine is also wonderful in all the recipes for using brine and whey.

—R

Eggs

Brown Eggs

When I was young my grandmother made brown eggs—huevos haminados, which is a very old Sephardic dish. No, they're not brown-shelled eggs, nor have they been dyed, at least not in this version. If you ask people about them, they will say to put onion skins or coffee grounds in with the water when you boil them, which really doesn't make them taste very nice. Or they will tell you these are roasted eggs, in which case an oven doesn't really work; you'd need a hearth to put them into hot coals, which gives you something similar, but usually a little charred and acrid. I suppose that's why my grandmother just boiled them—vigorously boiled them all day. Around 6 hours will work, but they're much better after 12, if you have the patience to keep adding water every hour or so.

The process completely transforms the eggs by caramelizing the sugars. The proteins break down, and the eggs become tender, nutty, and oddly reminiscent of roast fowl, which is not surprising given the source. The shape also becomes flattened on top as the egg loses mass overall. Eggs are among those few odd foods, like squid and good lamb, that should be cooked either very quickly or slowly forever.

The way to eat huevos haminados, always cold, is to flatten an egg between your two palms until it splits. Sprinkle on coarse sea salt and a few drops of lemon. Although this is the apotheosis of egg, you can take these a step further. More is more! Scoop out the yolks and mash them with a few drops of olive oil (not commercial mayo), and some cayenne pepper and salt. Pipe this mixture through a pastry bag fitted with a star tip back into the bottoms and dust with some more cayenne. Seriously bedeviled eggs, and people will have no idea how they were made. If you have less patience, go ahead and mash them up with a little mayo and spread on toast.

Another option is to put these eggs into a proper pickling brine, half salty water, half white vinegar, with some pungent spices like juniper, cardamom, or whole cumin. Whatever moves you. Leave them there for a few weeks, and you have pickled brown eggs. They go splendidly with dark hoppy beer, which brings out the nuttiness. I have never tasted anything like it on earth.

—K

Thousand-Year-Old Eggs

Making thousand-year-old eggs is among the scariest things I have ever tried at home. They're pretty frightening even bought at the store. If you have a great Asian grocery store like mine, there among the live bull frogs and balut (fertilized duck eggs), you'll find the thousand-year-old eggs, essentially an egg cured with lye. The smell is intensely ammoniac, and the color perfectly lurid, but they taste rather pleasant. They're especially nice chopped up in a salad or with an array of little nibblies.

To make them at home, take 6 duck or chicken eggs (or however many you want). In a bucket (with gloves!—this is seriously alkaline and will burn your skin) mix 2 or 3 pounds of white clay with a few handfuls of fine wood ash, a packet of cal (calcium hydroxide or slaked lime, which you can buy in a Mexican grocery), some moistened tea leaves (pu-er is perfect), and a handful

of salt. Mold the clay mixture around each egg (shell on, uncooked of course) and then wrap each in fallen bamboo fronds. (I have a lot of these; they drop as the bamboo grows in its first few weeks.) Rice bran is traditional or any kind of sturdy dry leaves should work, too. Put the bundles in a sealed clay jar and leave them somewhere, for 1,000 years.

Actually, 100 days should be enough; they will be very a terrifying bluish green and smell like horse piss, but otherwise perfectly edible. If you're lucky you'll get some delicate pine-needle patterns on the eggs as well.

—K

Ambergris

When you do culinary history, sometimes you come across an ingredient that just boggles the mind. The ancient Romans were pretty deranged—flamingo tongues, sows' wombs, and dormice were all standard fare. But I think seventeenth-century Europe beats them. Think of this as high Baroque cooking, with cloudbursts, cherubs, swags everywhere, and food garnished with perversities such as cockscombs (the squiggly things on roosters' heads) and testicles, marrow, gooseberries, and then the flavoring that tops them all: ambergris. Ambergris is a waxy glob that forms in the intestines of sperm whales, which they barf up. To start, it supposedly smells awful, but after tossing on the waves it takes on an ethereal perfumed fragrance, and indeed perfume is normally where it ends up. It's ridiculously expensive, but if you're intrepid and feeling profligate, look online and you can buy a little lump. My friend Deana swears by ambergris in chocolate, as did the great gourmand Brillat-Savarin. But I think the Baroque use is far more interesting. This comes from Bartolomeo Stefani's *L'Arte di ben cucinare* published in Mantua in 1662. It is essentially a kind of hollandaise with ambergris grated right in. It's marvelous on poached asparagus, as the author suggests, but also in a serious eggs Benedict, or even in place of a béarnaise on a delicate piece of steak. Don't be tempted to omit the sugar!

Butter Sauce with Ambergris

Take a pound of fresh butter, melted in a pan and add a half of a nutmeg powdered, a little clove powdered, four ounces of fine sugar, six egg yolks tempered with three ounces of lemon juice, and if you like perfume it with musk or ambergris, whatever pleases you; this works with dishes that are not long cooked like asparagus, artichokes, broccoli and various other things.

—K

6

Desserts

The very idea of banishing sweets to the end of a meal, with a separate course called dessert, is a relatively recent phenomenon. The tables would literally be deserted, stripped of linens and cutlery, before a final sweet course emerged. But before the late seventeenth century, every course would include sweets. Even the savory dishes contained sugar. It would be like having pie with your starter, cake with the main course, and then dessert with your dessert. For those of you who like this idea, we offer the following, to be consumed at every part of a meal.

Italian Ice

Italian ice and the whole tribe of sorbets have a long historical pedigree, whether they be made with snow trudged down from the mountains and flavored with sweet fruity syrup or the immediate ancestors of ice cream, chilled and churned in a bucket of icy water, whose temperature was lowered with saltpeter. My initial experience with such treats was not of the historical variety though. I once took a summer job driving an Italian-ice truck on the Jersey Shore. There were maybe a dozen fluorescent flavors in big tubs refrigerated at the back of the truck, and whenever someone hailed me down, I had to put the truck in park and go scoop the ices into little paper cups. The sugary syrup naturally soaked into my skin and after a few hours it made me *very* dizzy. The obnoxious tune that played over and over was hypnotizing. There were little sunburned children with sticky money chasing after the truck, a weird sugar buzzed psychedelic trip. I lasted 2 weeks.

You need not suffer such indignities to enjoy Italian ice though. In fact the original and traditional way of making it is much better. Notice this is not gelato, which uses cream, or a granita, which is just ice. The egg white makes the difference here, and you definitely do not need an ice cream maker, just a freezer, unless you prefer hiking up snowcapped mountains.

I used Meyer lemons because that's what I have in season during the winter in Stockton, California. The fruit is small but pretty intense and aromatic, so here's a delicious dessert that's simple to make and can be saved in the freezer until warmer weather arrives.

Take ½ bottle of dry rosé wine and 1 cup of raw brownish turbinado sugar. Heat to boiling until the sugar is all dissolved and then let cool. Grate the zest of 1 lemon, squeeze and strain the juice of 2 lemons and add to the zest. Mix this with the cooled wine in a bowl and put into the freezer. You will be deal-

ing with this in just a few minutes, so there's no need to seal it.

Next take 4 oranges and cut off the tops. (You can use lemons, too, of course.) Scoop out the flesh and juice with a spoon, leaving the peel and tops intact. Freeze these as your containers for the ice. Squeeze out the orange juice and add to the lemon-wine mixture and return to the freezer.

Every hour or so stir up the semifrozen mixture until you have a fine, grainy, and almost solid slush. This should take 5 or 6 hours. Next beat 1 egg white at room temperature with an infinitesimal pinch of salt until stiff peaks are formed. Fold this gently into the slushy ice and as quickly as you can, scoop into the empty orange shells, put on the tops and pop in the freezer. Let harden overnight. When you want to eat them, take them out of the freezer, let sit for a few minutes, and serve. If you want to keep them longer wrap the filled oranges in plastic wrap, and wait till summer.

—K

Apple Cider Doughnuts

When I was in college I spent a few weeks each year at the end of May working at a local orchard. It was a beautiful place, right on the site of the Battle of Monmouth and situated in the state park. There were a few odd jobs, like thinning peach trees—imagine being covered in peach fuzz in sweltering heat—and even worse, tying little mesh bags of human hair on saplings to keep the deer away. The hair came from a barbershop, so there were also cigarette butts and lollypop sticks mixed in. Most of the time, however, was spent picking strawberries. I spent weeks on hands and knees shuffling down each straw-covered row, filling up flats. They were delicious fat strawberries. The owners had an ingenious stratagem to keep us from eating them all. On the first day they said, "Eat as many as you want." I'm sure I ate several pounds on the first day. Just a few on the second. And by the third day the last thing I wanted to eat was a strawberry.

In my mind there was a certain Rousseauian pleasure in being close to the earth, laboring hard, and earning a mere $12 a day, which was consumed each night in drinks. It was tough, especially when the weather turned hot and humid. But the best part was midday; someone would come by with an ice cold jug of fresh apple cider and a paper bag of cider doughnut rejects. They were crunchy little nubbins, covered in cinnamon and sugar. I think the experience has spoiled me for life on store-bought doughnuts.

I have never been able to replicate those doughnuts exactly. Naturally the setting and back-breaking labor enhanced the flavor. And no recipe I've found has quite the zing. So I've messed with them. Also, traditionally these are fried in vegetable shortening, which apparently prevents them from soaking up oil and going soggy, but I just can't in good conscience use the stuff. So we'll go with lard. (Preferably rendered at home; a hydrogenated flavorless white block of lard is just as bad as shortening.) If that doesn't appeal to you, use vegetable oil.

Make a batter by creaming ½ stick of butter with ¾ cup of sugar. Add 1 capful of vanilla extract and a pinch of ground nutmeg. Then add 2 eggs, mixed in well, followed by 1½ cups of apple cider, the unpasteurized brown stuff, preferably from tart apples like Empire, Macoun, or Winesap. Or better yet use real hard cider, the alcohol evaporating as the doughnuts fry makes them super crisp. Then gradually mix in about 3 cups of whole wheat pastry flour, 2 tablespoons of baking powder, and a pinch of salt. Don't overmix. You want a fairly stiff batter, so add more flour if necessary.

Get a cast-iron skillet with a couple of inches of lard bubbling hot. Then drop in misshapen globs of batter from a kitchen spoon. The more irregular the better. Turn over and continue frying until brown. Place on a rack and immediately sprinkle with a 50–50 mix of cinnamon and sugar. Eat these treats as soon as you can get them into your mouth without getting burned. Chances are you will have a lot left over—put them in a bowl and sprinkle with Apple Jack (a splendid whiskey, which has been made just a few miles from the orchard mentioned earlier since the eighteenth century). Norman calvados will work fine, too. Serve these juicy spiked knobs with vanilla ice cream and pretend you are a colonial landowner.

—K

Hamantaschen

Though I might be accused of abjuring the faith of my ancestors, I shall be frank and unabashedly forthright: I've never liked hamantaschen. They are soft and greasy wads of dough formed into a triangle with a gob of jam in the middle. Like much of the best of Eastern European Jewish cooking it has either been co-opted by the food industry (weep for gefilte fish) or is made at home with such dull and uninspired ingredients (like margarine) that it is a pale shadow of its former hamishe self. (Ah, *hamishe* means "homey" in Yiddish.) I've tried the supposedly authentic prune and poppy seed versions but they left me wondering, What's all the fuss? I hate Purim, too.

One particular Purim I happened to be away in Paris, being the consummate flaneur, and wandered into the Jewish quarter of the Marais district. Schwartz's Deli; kosher butchers; and then, in a shop window, some hamantaschen of such unparalleled beauty that I had to try re-creating them (even though I never tasted them!). Most recipes you will find are so depressing. Oil, sugar, flour . . . some use butter and ask you to make pretty frilled margins. Nope, I had to wing it. And though I rarely believe in recipes, this worked so nicely, despite what sounds like a cacophony of ingredients, that I submit the following for your delectation. Let's call it Maple-Blood-Orange-Oat-Kumquat-Amarena Hamantaschen. Feel free to play with the ingredients in the dough and filling.

Take 1 stick of butter and cream with ¾ cup of fine maple sugar; add 1 egg and ¼ teaspoon of vanilla extract. Zest and then juice ½ of a blood orange and add to the mix. Next in a mortar or blender (if you must) grind 1 cup of rolled oats and 1 tablespoon of ground flaxseed until fine, add 1 cup of flour and 1 tablespoon of baking powder and work into a dough. Let dough chill in the fridge for 1 hour. Then roll out, cut circles with a small wineglass—you should get 30 to 40 circles. Place a tiny dollop of kumquat marmalade in the center and top with a cherry in syrup (your own, or Fabbri is fantastic). Resist the urge to use a maraschino. Then fold in three sides so you have a triangle (or Haman's hat) with the cherry peeking out in the middle and bake at 350°F for 25 minutes. Let cool. *Eat. Many.*

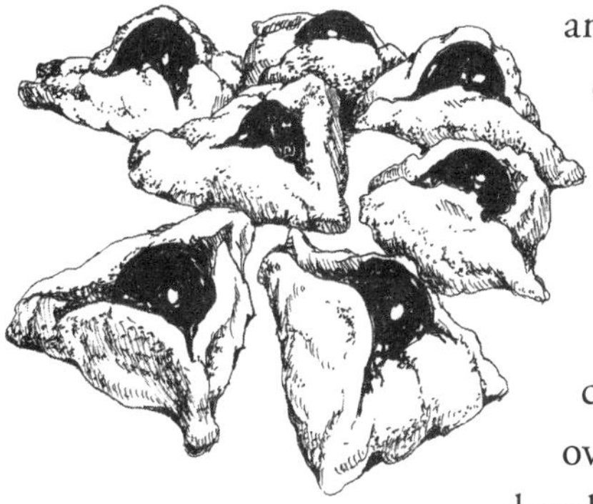

This same dough can be used to great effect with some caramelized onions spread evenly over the entire batch of rolled-out dough. The dough is then rolled up as for cinnamon rolls, cut into rounds to reveal the onions in a spiral, and then baked until crisp and brown. They make a wicked cocktail snack.

—K

Jasper of Milk

Take good fat milk and as much egg whites passed through a sieve, a bit of parsley chopped, a bit of white powder, seasoned with salt. Then put everything together and let it boil. And when it is cooked and you have stirred it well put it into a napkin to press and leave it to cool for about one day. Then cut in little slices and fry in butter. Serve hot with sugar on top and bring to the table and it looks like jasper.

This recipe, published in the anonymous sixteenth-century French *Livre fort excellent de cuysine* is typical of the "subtleties" that normally appeared at the end of a formal meal, clever devices that showcase the cook's wit and ingenuity. Jasper is a mottled green and white stone of great value and extremely difficult to sculpt. Thus relatively simple and inexpensive ingredients are transformed by culinary genius into something sublime. The white powder called for here is a frequently used combination of sugar, powdered ginger, and cinnamon. The final effect is both visually stimulating and delicious, a sweet-and-savory egg combination.

—K

Sugar Candy

I will readily admit to a lifelong fondness for candy, not chocolate or even candy bars—just bright-colored sugary junk. I was raised in an era when wealth was measured solely by one's personal stock of novelties such as Zotz, Jolly Ranchers, Bottle Caps, Pop Rocks, Razzles, and Pixy Stix. The further from anything even vaguely recognizable as food, the better, and if it exploded in your mouth, fizzed with caustic acid, or performed some gustatory prestidigitation, it was like gold. These hold little appeal for me today, and new outlandish candies have mostly replaced them, but I still find the simplest of boiled old-fashioned candies irresistible. As a species, we are hardwired to prefer sweetness from the moment we are born. Why should we ever be weaned from this biological predilection?

Historically sugar is also of utmost importance. In the late Middle Ages, when sugar first reached Europe in quantity from Asia, people were dumbstruck by both its flavor and its therapeutic possibilities. It was not merely a spoonful of sugar that helped the medicine go down, it *was* the medicine—and the base of countless cordials, syrups, julebs, and electuaries. By the sixteenth century it also became a universal flavoring, sprinkled liberally on practically every dish, even the savory ones. Sugar was molded into grand sculptures, and no meal was complete without a dish of comfits—that is, candies based on breath-sweetening spices. I need not mention that sugar plantations in the New World and the enslavement of millions of African to work them was the direct result of this European sweet tooth.

In this section we revisit those sugary candies that charmed our ancestors and rightly deserve to be made today. Many have descendants that are pale lifeless imitations of the original. One need only think of modern marshmallows, chewy red licorice, or the pathetic artificially sweetened pabulum known as bubble gum. Here are some real seriously flavored candies to tickle your palate.

Licorice

Licorice is one of those things you love or hate. I don't mean the twisted artificially flavored stuff they sell at movie theaters. We're talking about the real thing—the Dutchman's salty drop or even better Finnish salmiakki processed with ammonia. There's no better way to taste unfettered licorice than to chew on a dried root, don dreadlocks, and listen to reggae. But as candy, honestly the Italians and Spanish make the best licorice in the world. On trips I stock up on little tins. The ingredients should read *licorice* and nothing else, not even sugar. It is also the simplest and most ancient of candies to make, with profound medicinal virtues as well.

But first you must grow it. *Glycyrrhiza glabra*, apart from being one of the loveliest of terms to pronounce, means "sweet root" and was cultivated around the Mediterranean since ancient times. Oddly enough, licorice is a legume in the pea family and will produce pods if left to mature. If you live in a hot enough climate, it should be a snap. Just buy seeds and throw them in the ground as you would peas. In the fall, the plants should be 5 or 6 feet tall; just yank them up. The taproot and any smaller side roots are what you want. Wash and peel them, finely chop the yellow interior and put it in pot of water. Boil vigorously for at least 1 hour or more. Strain the solids and return the liquid to the pot and continue cooking gently until syrupy and thick. Pour this liquid onto a nonstick baking pan and either set out in the sun to dry or put in the oven at 100°F until it is thoroughly brittle. Break up the licorice into little pieces and store in an airtight jar. Its flavor will last forever, so parse it out judiciously.

—K

Sugar Plate

In the late sixteenth and early seventeenth centuries, diners were enamored of what they called "subtleties"—ingenious tricks whereby one food was disguised as another, fish molded as a fowl and marzipan shaped like fruit, one of the few surviving examples of these food illusions. Among these were sugar sculptures, and especially sugar plate. It is exactly what it sounds like: dishes and cups made from sugar paste, which can be eaten. The seventeenth-century gastronomic pundit Hugh Plat in his elegant little treatise *Delights for Ladies* describes his own sugar-plate techniques: "To make both marchpane paste and sugar plate, and cast the same in forms of sweetest grace, Each bird and foule so moulded from the life, and after cast in sweete compounds of arte, as if the flesh and forme which Nature gave, still remaine in every limb and part." To create this "rare and strange device" he instructs readers to make a plaster mold around an actual animal, a pigeon or rabbit, remove the animal, and then fill the mold with marzipan or sugar paste, which after being removed is decorated to look exactly like the living animal. "By this meanes a banquet may be presented in the forme of a supper." That is, dessert can be made of illusory supper dishes.

Ordinary plates are just as much fun. The only tool required is a mold, which can be simply a small wooden bowl or plate, oiled. Otherwise the sugar plate will be permanently lodged, as I found out after many experiments. This recipe is a simplified version of Plat's recipe. Start with 1 pound of sugar and 6 ounces of starch. You can use potato starch (though anachronistic), rice starch, or ideally wheat starch, if you can find it. It can be made by soaking flour and pouring off the liquid repeatedly. The starch sinks to the bottom. Then take a "pretty lump of the bignesse of a walnut of gumme tragagant, first steeped in Rose-water one night"—the gum can be bought at a cake-decorating shop or online. It normally comes in powdered form today, so you can skip the overnight soak and just moisten it with rose water. Mix the steeped gum with 1 egg white and roll between your fingers, gradually adding the sugar and starch until you have a malleable paste. You can form this by hand into whatever shape you like or roll it out on a board sprinkled with powdered sugar and set into your mold. Let dry several days and gently pry from the mold. At this point you can take natural food dye and paint on decorations. Blue looks very much like the cobalt in Delftware. Now delight the ladies.

(The taste, incidentally, will be unmistakably familiar to

people my age—it is identical to those chalky white candy cigarettes.)

—K

Molasses Candy/Theriac

Molasses candy is a really nasty sweet meant only for those with the most malevolent of palates. Its ancestry is quite noble, however, and ancient. It started as a dark bitter medicinal cure-all and poison antidote known as theriac, which included over sixty ingredients, among which were opium, myrrh, cinnamon, and other drugs. The idea was that one nasty poison drives out all others. In England this came to be called treacle, which evolved into a cooking ingredient, essentially a sugar by-product, which happens to be a lighter, less aggressive cousin of molasses. I spotted this recipe on a piece of paper at Tudor Place, a historic house in Georgetown, and scribbled it down excitedly as best I could. Practically every nineteenth-century cookbook has a version, which makes perfect sense because there was a surfeit of molasses in those days. In 1919, an explosion in a molasses-processing factory in the North End neighborhood of Boston sent the boiling syrup into the streets, killing twenty-one people. This is a diverting but very dangerous recipe.

Here is the simplest version I tried, which uses only molasses. Recipes including sugar came out lighter in flavor and color. First boil 1 cup of molasses and 1 tablespoon of butter with a touch of vanilla extract. Stir constantly to the hard crack stage. (Test a drop in a bowl of ice water until it comes out crunchy.) Then add ½ tablespoon of vinegar and ¼ teaspoon of baking powder. Turn out onto a buttered cookie sheet. Now before it cools plunge your tender, naked (and well-buttered) hands right in and start pulling like taffy into long strands, and keep folding over. Then before it becomes solid, stretch one final time into thin ropes and twist them. By now your hands will be blistered and red, and you will be whining in abject pain, unless you wimp out and go with gloves. Let the candy cool and then crack into desired lengths. They go very nicely with bourbon. Do not offer to children; they will hate you for it.

—K

Butterscotch Taffy

Using the same procedure as for molasses candy but substituting sugar, you can make a lovely hard, shiny golden candy. If you pull it and twist it just before it hardens, it looks exactly like Goldilocks's silken tresses.

In the event that you actually want to be able to pull this without burning your hands, boil just to the soft crack stage. This version is not quite as visually arresting, but it has a truly sophisticated flavor that reminds me of butterscotch, but really nice and chewy. Not like the bright, artificially flavored, soft saltwater taffy you find at the boardwalk. This is the real stuff that rips the fillings from your teeth. Use 2 cups of raw demarara sugar, ¾ cup of water, 2 tablespoons of butter, 2 tablespoons of rice flour (cornstarch works, too), ¼ cup of dark wild flower honey, ½ teaspoon of ground cinnamon, and ¼ teaspoon of cream of tartar. Mix these all together, and heat without stirring to the soft crack (270°F) stage. A bowl of ice water works fine for testing if you don't have a candy thermometer. Soft crack is when a drop of the hot syrup in ice water is still a little malleable. Pour the candy out on a greased cookie sheet and let cool thoroughly. Then pull for 10 to 15 minutes. It lightens in color like magic. Form into long ropes and cut them with buttered scissors. The most interesting thing about this candy, although jaw-breaking at first, is that if you leave it out uncovered for a few weeks, it becomes soft, with the same texture as butter mints.

—K

Gum

I think there must be some instinctive urge to chew inherited from our hominid ancestors. It's so satisfying to get your teeth around a hunk of gum, a spicy betel quid, a green lump of khat, or pinch of coca leaves. In the nineteenth century, spruce gum was all the rage, and even when I was a kid, you could still find Kennebec spruce gum from Maine, little dark globs, for sale in historic houses. It's now gone, so I suggest making your own. First find a spruce, which is a Christmas tree, easily identified by its needles, which emerge singly from each nodule and have four sides. If you happen to find a pine, that's fine, too. They're all edible. Just look for dried hard sap that has poured from a wound in the tree. Pick it off, and don't worry if there's bark or needles in it. Take a double thickness of aluminum foil and poke a few holes in it. Put the sap inside and close it up. Place this on a rack in your barbecue. You can use your oven instead, if you don't mind resiny incense in the house. Underneath the sap put a foil-lined pan. Heat to about 300°F. The sap will melt through and drip into the pan. With oven mitts on, squeeze the foil to extract every last drop. Let the sap cool a little and while still warm roll it into a log shape. When completely cool snap these into bite-size pieces. Dust with powdered sugar. When you first bite on a piece it will shatter and crumble; just chew for a minute until the mixture comes to body temperature, and it will be a perfectly resiny chew that amazingly never loses its flavor or texture. It can even be saved and chewed again—the original Everlasting Gob-stopper. Now you should understand why Becky Thatcher lets Tom Sawyer have a turn chewing her spruce gum, but wants it back again after.

—K

Mastika Glyko

Another irresistible gum, the most prized of all, comes from the lentisk tree, which grows on the Greek island of Chios. Our word *masticate* comes from this gum, and Christopher Columbus traded in it before setting off to Asia for spices. It is used in a variety of confections, the most arresting of which is called mastika glyko, alias βανίλια υποβρύχιο, which means "vanilla submarine," not to be confused with the similar-sounding song by the Beatles or with anything that actually contains vanilla. This doesn't. Take 1 cup of water and 1 cup of sugar and 1 teaspoon of rose water. Boil this in a pot to the firm ball stage, which is 240° to 250°F. If like me you have an aversion to thermometers, just put a drop of the syrup into a bowl of ice water and when a little sugar ball holds together but is still a little squishy, remove the pot from the stove. (Remember this stuff is so hot it will sear through flesh, so don't be tempted to taste it!) Add a few drops of lemon juice and 1 teaspoon of finely crushed mastic. You can find this at a Greek or Middle Eastern grocery, or online. Beat it rigorously with a wooden spoon until it's shiny and white and firm. The moment your traveling guests arrive, offer a spoonful of this in a glass of cold water, hence the nickname "submarine." It is perfectly sublime and invigorating, and yes you do chew and swallow it, in case you're wondering.

7

Brewing and Distillation

Social lubricant, a means of winding down after a long day at work, or the perfect accompaniment to a meal, alcohol is inextricably entwined with civilized life. Scientists have also discovered that it not only does not kill brain cells but in a certain sense clears out the stuffed mental filing cabinets crammed with minutiae, letting us focus on the important things in life. Most cultures have used alcohol in celebratory rituals because it brings us closer to divinity, helping us loosen those tight coils that bind us to daily rush and riot, effacing a sense of self and ultimately uniting us with the gods. What better way to honor the deities than letting natural processes transform simple fruits into a substance that is truly magical?

Mead

The simplest and probably the oldest of all fermented beverages is mead. It makes itself. If you add water to honey and leave it open, you will eventually have mead as wild yeast converts the sugars into alcohol. A few little tricks and you will be able to make really good mead. We are not talking about sweet mead. It should be amber colored, dry, and slightly fizzy. You don't suppose Beowulf and his Geats in the great mead hall were sipping some dainty swill? It has to be strong, refreshing, and guzzled from a horn. So start with a dark full-flavored honey, a 2-pound jar. Mix it with 8 times the amount of water, and add a packet of wine yeast, specifically designed for champagne is preferable. That will be enough for 2 gallons of mead. Pour this into some gallon jugs and fit the tops with airlocks. They cost a couple of dollars online, but make all the difference. An airlock is just a plastic vial that holds water, keeping out the air while letting the bubbles escape. You stick the lock into a cork and that goes into the bottle. After about 2 weeks the mead will be bone dry. Cap it, keep in a cool place and let it mellow. It resembles beer more than anything else.

With these very basic instructions you can make some lovely drinks out of just about anything. Think of it not so much as wine making, for which you squeeze the juice of grapes and let it ferment, but as making fruit-flavored low-alcohol drinks based on sugar. For example, a few pints of strawberries crushed in a sugar water solution, with the same yeast and airlocks, makes a lovely rosé that one might even mistake for wine were not the aroma deeply strawberried. You'll probably want to strain it before bottling though. The same goes for peaches. Flowers can be tossed in as well. Of course you've heard of dandelion wine; elderberry and even nettles make a delightful quaff.

—K

Cider

Colonial America was awash in hard cider. Apples grew easily; remember Johnny Appleseed? The best way to preserve them was and still is fermentation. If you can find fresh unpasteurized apple cider, leave it on the counter for a few days and it will ferment on its own. For a more refined product, it's best to buy some commercial yeast (champagne or white wine yeast works well) and a few airlocks. Use the tartest, gnarliest apples you can

find, not Red Delicious! If you are going for volume, a 5-gallon plastic fermentation tub is ideal, or a glass carboy. I often use gallon jugs, glass, or pottery.

The real challenge with cider making is the crushing and pressing. If you have a meat grinder, you can grind quartered apples. It makes a mess, but works. Just be sure it's stainless steel or you'll have really dirty-looking, metallic-tasting cider. Bashing them in a mortar is even messier, but a lot of fun. If you are so inclined, a juicer is the quickest and easiest. Beyond that there's a lot of expensive professional equipment for large volumes. At home 10 to 20 pounds of apples is perfectly manageable. Crush them and then put them in batches into a sturdy, impeccably clean dish towel and wring out the juice. You won't be able to get it all, but no matter. Compost the remains. Pitch in the yeast, a third of a packet per gallon is plenty, or go au naturel if you prefer and skip the yeast. Let it ferment for a couple of weeks. If you like, siphon off the clear juice from the top once the solids have settled. Then wait. The longer you can keep it around, the mellower it will be. Wait at least a month or so before trying it. Serve lightly chilled. It will be very dry, tart (we hope), and remarkably thirst quenching. Call it "scrumpy." Erp, 'tis that.

—K

Birch Beer

From the time I was seven my parents sent me to a sleepaway camp in the Pocono Mountains. I loved being away in the woods, and I assume they loved quiet summers to themselves. Among the nicest things about living in the woods is that you learn about plants, both the poison ivy to avoid and the good things to eat, like tiny lemony clover (which we also smoked!) and fresh blueberries, crushed and fermented into wine. (Okay, so I was a derelict at a young age.) But of all these, the Proustian moment for me is the flavor of real birch beer. Just strip some bark with the greenish part beneath from brown birch, not all the way around or you'll kill the tree. Add it to a pot of boiling water, sweeten to taste, and let steep. Strain and drink hot or leave it around in an open pitcher for a few weeks. It will definitely ferment, and if you then cap it in an old soda bottle, it will get fizzy, too. I have never tried to make it using a more sophisticated method, but I'm sure it can be done. Sassafras root works the same way. Just look for mitten-shaped leaves with two or three fingers. Dig up a small plant with root intact. Clean, peel, and steep the same way as for birch. This is the original root beer, by the way. The leaves can also be dried and ground into filé powder for your gumbo.

—K

Hooch

The origins of distillation are shrouded in mystery, quite intentionally so, as the procedures were part of a larger alchemical enterprise, meant to be kept secret among a few select practitioners of the spagyrical art (also known as magi). Some scholars point to classical roots, and it does seem that the ancients performed a crude kind of distillation by placing a rag over a vessel of boiling wine and then squeezing out the liquid. This subtle concentrated form of wine was called spirits—much like blood, which was thought to be distilled in the brain to form the spirits that animated our bodies and gave rise to thought. Because wine and blood were considered analogs, so too were these two forms of spirits. And alcohol, by logical extension, could be used to prolong life because it supplied exactly what the body needed without the arduous process of digestion.

Distillation as we know it was most likely invented in the medieval Muslim world and then transported to Europe, where the still was further perfected. By the fifteenth century, as one can see in distillation manuals like that of Hieronymus Braunschweig, the standard still was just a very simple clay vessel with a long "nose" extending in an arc and finishing in a small opening. It's basically just a retort flask. One merely filled this with wine and set it in a dish full of sand to steady the bottom, and placed the dish on hot coals. The steam that forms goes up the nose, condenses when it meets the cooler part of the vessel and the spirits issue from the end, into another vessel. A modern still follows this same basic procedure, the only difference being it is made of copper, can be set directly over the heat source and it comes apart for cleaning. You can buy a beautiful three-liter alembic still made in Portugal by Al-Ambiq for around $250. Well worth the investment if you plan to make your own hooch.

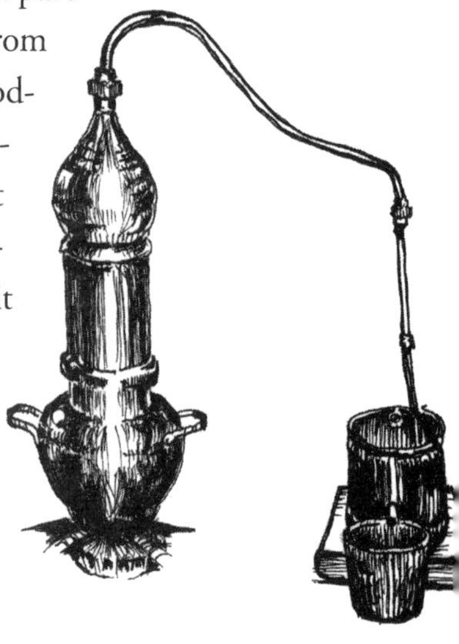

Before we start, you must understand that distilling alcohol is strictly illegal in the United States, and you must never under any circumstances try to do it. I explain the process here for purely historical purposes. And if you must make your own potcheen, then *run like the devil from the excise man. Keep the smoke from rising, Barney!* and don't forget that our founding fathers were knee-deep in their own homemade whiskey. When Alexander Hamilton tried to tax it in the 1790s, he provoked the Whiskey Rebellion.

The easiest spirit to make is the product of wine, the easiest alcoholic drink to make. Get some good ripe grapes that haven't been sprayed. The amount is up to you. I can usually fill my big stockpot with grapes from the backyard, and that's a nice amount to deal with if you have no equipment. Crush the grapes by hand, or feet if you like that sort of thing. You can go au naturel for fermentation, which I like a lot, or pitch in a packet of commercial wine yeast. Normally then you'll have to sterilize everything with campden tablets, then add the yeast, so you get only the strain you want. Either way, push the cap of skins and fermenting must down every day or twice a day for about 2 weeks. The mixture will bubble nicely and smell like wine. It does actually make itself with little intervention on your part.

Next, strain the mix through a sieve and to remove most of the wine, put a few handfuls of the skins and seeds into a sturdy (and clean) dishcloth and wring out the juice. This will take a while. You won't get it all, but the only other option is a press. If you like you can put the wine into bottles or a glass carboy topped with an airlock. Otherwise your wine will most likely turn to vinegar if kept very long exposed to air. How long you leave it at this stage is up to you, but over a few weeks you will see it clarify. Because you won't be drinking this as wine, it really doesn't matter how long it's left or how refined it is.

I once filled a big pottery jug with my own wine and pushed it to the back of a cabinet, upright, and found it there 5 years later. I expected it to be rotten and sour; instead, the red pigment and solids had all settled to the bottom and I poured out a golden clear oxidized nectar, not at all unlike the best sherry I've ever tasted. I drank one glass and distilled the rest. Unbelievably good.

Take your wine—or you can just buy a jug of plonk—and put it in the vessel of your alembic. Seal the joint with a rye flour dough; rye expands and won't crack like wheat dough. In the copper cylinder at the far end of your still that holds the coil, place ice and a little cup at the end of the nozzle. It's an ingenious device; from a spigot on one side, the alcohol that condenses in the coil will pour out, from the other the overflow of ice water. Make sure you put another cup on the other side. Heat the alembic on the stove full throttle. When wine reaches about 80°C (176°F), it turns to gas, before the water, so keep the heat below 100°C (212°F). The gas travels up and through the copper coil or snake, and when it hits the ice water it turns back into liquid. Alcohol. There are of course much more sophisticated and scientific ways to do this, but this works perfectly at home.

This process is not, of course, just for hooch; there are also a slew of medical nostrums and perfumes that you can distill at home. In the seventeenth and eighteenth centuries, especially on rural estates, these would commonly be made at home.

—K

Rose Water

> *Earthlier happy is the rose distill'd; Than that which withering on the virgin thorn, Grows, lives and dies in single blessedness.*
>
> —Shakespeare, *A Midsummer Night's Dream*

I have to agree with the Bard. But to make rose water you do need a *lot* of roses, and they can't be sprayed. Be sure to remove the white part as well; it's bitter. You also have to pound the rose petals to extract juice, and as you can expect, you only get a few drops from each flower, which is why Shakespeare also says in Sonnet VI: "Then let not winter's ragged hand deface, / In thee thy summer, ere thou be distilled: / Make sweet some vial; treasure thou some place, / With beauty's treasure, ere it be self-kill'd." Don't expect more than a tiny vial's worth, but it will last in a way the rose will not.

Hugh Plat's little book *Delights for Ladies* (1628) offers numerous typical recipes for rose water. This aromatic liquid was used as perfume, a cooling medicine for fevers and as a cooking ingredient. The process of distillation can take place either in a balneo (like the retort flask) a still, or a limbeck—that is, an alembic. Plat instructs:

> *Macerate the Rose in his own juice, adding thereto, being temperately warme, a convenient proportion either of yeast or ferment: leave them a few daies in fermentation, til they have gotten a strong and heady smell, beginning to incline toward vinegar then distill them in balneo in glass bodies luted to their helmes (happely a Limbeck will do better . . .) and drawe so long as you finde any sent of the Rose to come: then redistill of rectifie the*

same so often till you have purchased a perfect spirit of the Rose. You may also ferment the juice of Roses only, and after distill the same.

Now you are wondering what to do with this. A dab behind each ear, but then you risk being nibbled. The essence is delightful in desserts, especially those with almonds, but do not hesitate to be more emboldened. Savory dishes with a hint of rose are remarkably seductive, chicken with warm spices, and even lamb. Just be sure to add it at the end. Unlike Middle Eastern rose water you can purchase, and which is very good, just a few drops of this go a long way.

—K

Rossolis

Culinary history is filled with fascinating mysteries. I love how recipes change over time, sometimes substituting an ingredient that coincidentally sounds similar to the original. This seems to be the case with a cordial drink called rossolis. The name comes from the Latin *ros solis*, meaning "dew of the sun." It's a plant, a terrifying one in fact, with fine hairs that exude little sticky dewdrops on the end. Bugs that land on them are captured, then the tentacle-like shoot curls around and digests the bug. Gervase Markham, writing in the early seventeenth century, recorded a recipe that uses the plant, gathered without touching or washing the leaves; soaked in aquavit; then sweetened with sugar, licorice, and dates; and then distilled. It makes you strong and lusty. By the end of that century, this particular plant seems to have been replaced with roses (which just sound similar). The modern descendant is the Italian rosolio, which is a sweet rose-flavored cordial. In the late seventeenth century, any aromatic flower could be used, and it was apparently a favorite of Louis XIV. Audiger gives a recipe in his 1692 book, *La Maison Réglée.*

Essentially he says take whatever flower is in season and soak the petals with no leaves in water until the aroma is absorbed. (You want mostly petals and just enough water to cover.) Remove the petals and then add a pint of eau de vie (that's just clear alcohol) and sugar. Then he suggests adding distilled anise spirit (which is basically pastis or ouzo) and cinnamon spirit (which you can find in any liquor store among the flavored schnapps). If possible you will want to distill your own versions of these, but the following option is much more interesting: grains of amber (that is, ambergris) and musk blended with sugar. Audiger explains that you take 4 grains of amber, which is a specific pharmaceutical weight. Because 1 grain weighs exactly 0.06 gram, you'll need 0.24 gram or 0.008465750856 ounce. Okay, just use a pinch, along with 2 grains of musk. That's a substance found in a gland of an Asian musk deer, once widely used in perfumery and now quite illegal. But if you're intrepid, the real thing can be found. This is mixed with sugar the size of an egg, all reduced to a fine powder. The fine powder is used to perfume the rossolis.

When fresh flowers are out of season you can also use this mixture to perfume hypocras, which Audiger makes with white wine (such as Muscat, Rhine, or Champagne), citrus juice and peel, cinnamon, cloves, mace, coriander, and white pepper. He clarifies the mixture, but I think it's delightful just strained and then sweetened with the musky ambered sugar.

—K

Some Mixed Drinks

I began to mix drinks much younger than most people, around age fifteen or so. It was partly because I learned to like liquor at my best friend's house, whose parents drank like fish. I began to experiment at my house, where my parents drank nothing at all, but always had a closet stocked with excellent booze given as presents. I recall many a high school party at my place with a few friends, polishing off a bottle of Remy Martin or Hennessy XO. Spoiled me for life. We got it in our minds to mix outrageously good liquor with fruit juices, inventing drinks that might have been conjured up at nineteenth-century colonial outposts by desperate civil servants. A Dutchman mixing gin with coconut milk and lime in Jakarta (awfully good) or a Frenchman drinking cognac with hot apple cider and a dash of maple syrup in seventeenth-century Quebec (spectacular). The best of all these perversities, as odd as it sounds, was especially designed for Christmas, when oranges are in season: the Glorious Guyana, British Empire, circa 1820.

Take 2 shots of excellent Scotch whisky, single malt and peaty. Add the juice of 1 freshly squeezed orange, and 1 banana. Blend with a little crushed ice, add a few drops of angostura bitters, and serve in a highball. Consume many.

Another arresting combination for those of you with a yearning for wormwood is called the Opal Eyeball. It is designed to help you see into the future. Begin with a capacious glass ¾ full of real French Champagne. Add to it slowly 1 jigger of Suisse La Bleue Absinthe, the real stuff (my favorite is Clandestine or Enigma). Then drop in a single peeled fresh lychee. The drink bubbles and louches, becoming opalescent, and the texture of the lychee is perfectly obscene.

For everyday drinking, there is nothing like a good Manhattan though. If you can distill your own bourbon, all the better; if not there is such remarkably good stuff out there that you should not be embarrassed to purchase some. But do make all the rest yourself. I mean take fresh cherries and soak them in a syrup made of boiled-down cherry juice, sugar, a little booze, and a few drops of almond extract, which really brings out the flavor. Make your own vermouth with good red wine fortified with eau de vie and steeped with any herbs you like—I am partial to fennel, tarragon, and a touch of rue. But use whatever you have growing. Bitters are easy as well: Steep citrus peels (without the white pith) in grain alcohol, and flavor with spices such as nutmeg, star anise, or licorice root. My preference leans toward the licorice family, but use any combination you like. When the bourbon combines with the cherry, herbal vermouth, and spicy bitters, the combination is nothing less than revelatory. You will never want another standard mass-produced maraschino-topped Manhattan again.

—K

8

Nostrums and Household Stuffe

Let me be quite clear. This is one of the oddest and most dangerous chapters in the whole book. It covers chemicals from the astringent tannic acid of oak galls (for making ink) to highly caustic lye (for making soap). It advocates for cleaning your bathroom with symbiotic colonies of yeast and bacteria, and then touts the sweet symbolism of making wedding rings from silver quarters. Appropriately for such a chapter, you will even find directions for making a proper witch's broom.

This is one of the most fun ways to approach domesticity. It's a zany experiment, steeped in tradition and magic, and quite unlike the starchy and oppressive tedium of either 1950s housekeeping or today's infomercials.

Kombucha: Growing Your Own Mother and Brewing It for Refreshment or Utility

As a fizzy, refreshing fermented nonalcoholic beverage, kombucha has lately taken the world by storm and found its way into even the dustiest corner stores in San Francisco. This isn't its first resurgence. People have been brewing kombucha and touting its miraculous healing powers for a long time. In fact, it had its big debut in North America after World War I: Picture flappers sipping kombucha. And yet somehow it always seems like a recent alternative health fad.

I'm not going to bother with the controversy over the health benefits of kombucha. It's a mysterious, ancient elixir fermented with a thick rubbery "mushroom" (the mother), which is actually a symbiotic colony of bacteria and yeast (also called a SCOBY). Nobody has ever found a kombucha SCOBY in the wild, but it entered recorded history around 250 BCE in China. The main thing is, it's a delicious, nonsoda, (mostly) nonalcoholic, tart, fizzy, refreshing beverage.

Here's the other thing, though. Home-brewed kombucha is one of the least expensive ways to make vinegar. Its only ingredients are sugar and tea, and if you let it ferment long enough, you'll get a highly acidic liquid, useful for all the purposes acidic liquids are good for, like cleaning windows, rinsing hair, and making salad dressing.

The common wisdom is that to make your own kombucha, you have to buy a kombucha mother for a lot of money online or acquire one from your housemate's boyfriend, who got it from a girl on Craigslist in exchange for a ride to Portland. Sadly, the girl on Craigslist may have a subpar kombucha mother. It's hard to tell, but not all kombucha mothers are the same. A neglected kombucha mother, or any of its descendants, will fail to produce delicious, fizzy, happy kombucha—and it may even breed fruit flies.

Commercial kombucha brewers work with very high-quality kombucha mothers. You can propagate a high-quality kombucha mother of your own with just a bottle of raw kombucha from your favorite kombucha brand, a little care, some sugar, and good black tea. Yes, you can use nothing more than a bottle of store-bought kombucha as a starter for your own never-ending supply of kombucha.

Here's why: Every bottle of raw kombucha has very small strands of kombucha mother in it. Your job is to feed those strands until they form a strong kombucha mother. Too much food, and the kombucha won't be strong enough to culture the substrate, and it will mold. Too little food, and it won't grow.

Growing the Mother

First, select an excellent bottle of plain or gingered kombucha. It should have as many yeasty filaments floating in it as possible, and it *must* be raw. Heat kills kombucha. You can drink some of the kombucha if you like—just leave all of the sediment and stringy bits in the bottle, and at least ½ cup of liquid. Next, ready the kombucha food.

In a small saucepan, heat 1 cup of water to boiling. Add 2 tablespoons white sugar, and return the liquid to a boil until the sugar is dissolved. Turn off the heat and add 1 bag of organic black tea (or 1 tablespoon of loose leaf) and let the mixture cool at room temperature until it no longer feels the slightest bit warm to the touch. Remove the tea bag or strain the tea. Pour all the contents of the kombucha bottle into the sugar–tea mixture: the sediment, the ½ cup of kombucha liquid, and the stringy things (these will turn into the kombucha mother!), and put it all in a glass quart or pint jar. Cover the jar with a cloth and a tight rubber band to keep bugs out, and place it in a warm, dark, safe spot. Note that the kombucha liquid is necessary to keep the mixture sufficiently acidic. If the liquid is not acidic, mold will grow.

Keep an eye on the kombucha. In a few days or a week, it should start to grow a thin film over the surface. The film will thicken and become the kombucha mother. If any mold appears, discard everything and start over—but that shouldn't even be a possibility if you have enough acid in the liquid.

After 1 or 2 weeks, when the film is about ⅛ inch thick, you'll need to give the mix another little boost of food. It's not yet strong enough to culture a lot of kombucha for you to drink; right now it's just growing.

This time, make 1 quart of tea. Heat 4 cups of water to a boil, add ⅓ cup of sugar, and steep with 2 tea bags or 2 tablespoons of loose black tea. When the liquid cools completely, remove the tea leaves, put the baby kombucha and all the liquid and sediment in a large glass jar or bowl with the tea. Cover it tightly and watch it carefully. The kombucha mother should thicken significantly over the space of 2 weeks. When the mother is between ¼ and ½ inch thick, you can use it to make yourself a batch of kombucha.

Brewing Kombucha for Refreshment

Bring 3 quarts of filtered water to a boil. (If your water is chlorinated and you don't have a filter, leave the water sitting uncovered overnight to evaporate the chlorine.) Add 1 cup of sugar and return to a boil until dissolved; turn off the heat and add 4 tea bags (or 4 tablespoons loose leaf) black tea. Let cool completely to room temperature. Remove the tea bags or leaves, and put the liquid in a 1-gallon glass jar. Pour in 1 or 2 cups of finished kombucha liquid from the last batch (to keep everything acidic) and place the entire kombucha mother on top. It's okay if it sinks. Cover it securely with cloth and a rubber band, and place it in a warm, dark cupboard for 7 to 10 days. A new kombucha baby will grow on the surface of the liquid.

When the kombucha baby is ⅛ to ¼ inch thick, taste the kombucha. If it doesn't taste too sweet, you can harvest the liquid, leaving 1 or 2 cups in the bottom of the jar with the mother. You can give the baby kombucha away or just keep it in the jar along with the original mother. If you want continuous kombucha production, you can start brewing a second batch with the mother immediately, or just leave the mother in the liquid until you next need it. It keeps quite well for many months, if the jar is stored in a dark, cool cupboard and covered securely with fine cloth to keep out bugs.

At this point, the liquid you harvested will be flat. To get it fizzy, you'll need to put it through a secondary fermentation in airtight containers. Put 1 teaspoon of sugar in the bottom of each 16-ounce bottle or jar (or the proportionate amount) and fill it with kombucha to within ½ inch of the top. Cap all the bottles securely—any ordinary screw-cap or swing-top bottle will work, so long as it keeps out air—and put the bottles in the cupboard for 1 week. If the room temperature is very warm, you might want to check them earlier to prevent any explosions.

You can also add flavorings when you bottle the kombucha: ginger, spices, raisins, or a few tablespoons of fruit juice. Or perhaps you want to brew your own medicinal tonics. The acid and weak alcohol content of kombucha are better at extracting the active components of many medicinal herbs than is plain water. Most anything you might brew as a tea can be added to a bottle of kombucha during its secondary fermentation, with potent results. For example, a few tablespoons of dried dandelion root per bottle create a wonderfully bitter liver tonic.

Once the bottles are fizzy, store them in the refrigerator to slow down their fermentation. While kombucha is quite delicious and refreshing, don't guzzle it, or you'll find yourself with a stomachache instead of boundless health.

Brewing Kombucha for Utility

If you let the kombucha go on fermenting for several weeks before harvesting the liquid, it will become unpalatably acidic. It will be quite useful for other purposes, however. Although kombucha produces other acids in addition to acetic acid (vinegar), it works well as a vinegar substitute that requires very little effort or expense to make.

Since virtually all of the sugar has been fermented into acid at this point, you can safely harvest the kombucha liquid into bottles, where it will keep for months at room temperature. Then your kombucha mother will be freed up to produce other batches of drinkable kombucha. Or you can keep the liquid in the original fermenting jar; just pour off strong kombucha as you need it.

Strong kombucha is an excellent cleanser for kitchen and bathroom surfaces. It kills mold and mildew on contact. If you wet newspapers with it, you can use it to clean windows and mirrors, too.

In the kitchen, kombucha works very much like cider vinegar. It's weaker than wine vinegar, but you can use it in dressings and to brighten up soups. If it's sufficiently strong, you can even use it to pickle.

My grandmother used to rinse her hair with cider vinegar, which smooths and conditions hair quite nicely. Lately I've been using strong kombucha for the same purpose. I put a few tablespoons in ½ cup of water with a drop of essential oil. After shampooing and rinsing, I dip the ends of my hair in it and pour the rest over the top of my head, then rinse it out thoroughly a minute later. The vinegar smell does not linger, though acidic rinses do make hair slightly more vulnerable to sun-bleaching (much like that lemon-juice-in-the-sun bleaching trick).

An acidic rinse works equally well for nonhuman animal fibers. After washing and rinsing, soak a wool garment in a basin of water with 1 cup of vinegar or kombucha for 15 minutes. It softens and conditions wool beautifully. Squeeze out the vinegar water and rinse again. Do keep the vinegar well diluted, of course, especially when rinsing delicate woolens or brilliant dyes. Fine materials like merino and silk are plenty soft on their own.

—R

Soap

The rise of industrial vegetable oils has completely changed the content of our soap (not to mention our diets). A hundred years ago or so, the most abundant fats around were animal fats, like tallow and lard. It was much easier to raise a pig or two than to plant a field of soy or rapeseed and extract the oil. Getting oil out of temperate-climate seeds requires heavy industrial machinery, powerful solvents, and lots of bleaching and deodorizing to make the oils smell decent. In fact, vegetable oils are sometimes even saponified (turned into soap) first, before getting centrifuged to purify the oil. Warm-climate oils, like coconut and olive, can be extracted without so much fuss, which explains why they have a much older tradition of use.

Modern industrial production means that vegetable oils are now quite cheap and ubiquitous, while our livestock has been bred to produce less fat. In this environment, I can hardly bring myself to turn precious animal fats into soap. I would much rather cook with my bacon drippings and use cheap sunflower oil for my soap.

The process of making your own soap involves dangerous substances, dramatic chemical reactions, and creativity. It's an excellent way to generate gifts for a large number of people. I write here about the simplest cold-process method for making soap, which requires a month or so of curing time, but you can also experiment with hot-process soap for instant gratification.

To make soap, you'll need nonreactive (glass, stainless steel, or plastic) containers and utensils for everything that comes in contact with the lye. That means two bowls, a stirring spoon, and a whisk or immersion blender. You'll also want an accurate scale for weighing out your fats, water, and lye. And you'll want to have the space and time to keep people and animals out of your kitchen when you're working.

The first recipe I give here is for a basic olive oil and coconut oil soap—ingredients easily found in a grocery store. You can find the lye at a hardware store. Just be careful to buy 100 percent lye (sodium hydroxide) with no added ingredients. Rooto is one such brand I've found quite easily.

Avoid tinkering with soap recipes willy-nilly. Different fats require different amounts of lye to saponify. If the lye-to-fat ratio drops too low, you'll have greasy soap or soap that never comes together. If the lye-to-fat ratio gets too high, you'll have the worse problem of caustic soap that burns your skin. Furthermore, different fats have different properties in soap—hardness, latheriness, and so on. That doesn't mean you shouldn't develop new soap recipes! You can find helpful lye calculators online (try soapCalc.net) to help you generate new recipes without gambling with the lye.

Most soap recipes are also superfatted, meaning they include a buffer of excess fat beyond what will absorb all the lye. Most soap is about 5 percent superfatted, meaning it has 5 percent excess fat by weight. If soap weren't superfatted, it would feel unusually harsh, like washing your hands with laundry detergent.

Olive Oil Soap

Here's a recipe for soap that will smell subtly of whichever olive oil you use for it. I like the grassy sunny aroma of cheap-but-flavorful olive oil, but you can use a very bland olive oil if you'd prefer. Likewise, I use refined coconut oil to avoid an overpowering coconut scent.

Coconut oil also makes a highly detersive soap, so much so that it needs to be generously superfatted at 15 percent. You can also add up to 1 ounce of fragrance oils without disrupting the recipe. This recipe makes about 1 pound of soap. You can easily scale it if you have large enough mixing containers.

Before you start, prepare a soap mold. For this amount of soap, I use a cardboard tea box lined with parchment paper. The soap will be thick enough by the time you pour it into the mold that you won't need to worry about leaks.

I like to confine my soap making to a cleared-out, clean sink by an open window. Remember that lye can easily give you chemical burns in both dry and liquid form, and it produces unhealthy vapors. Wear elbow-length rubber gloves, and celebrate this excuse to don some steampunk goggles.

Use a designated clean, nonreactive container for mixing the lye and water. Try something plastic out of your recycling bin. Tare the scale accordingly and weigh out 6 ounces of purified water, preferably distilled or at least very filtered. Set the container of water in the bottom of your sink. In a new nonreactive container, measure out 2 ounces of dry lye. Slowly pour the lye into the water and stir with a large plastic spoon. Try to avoid breathing the fumes. It will start to heat up as the lye and water react. Let the lye–water mixture cool while you prepare the oils.

Combine 4 ounces of coconut oil and 12 ounces of olive oil in a small saucepan. Gently heat to melt the coconut oil.

Now you want to get the temperatures of the lye water and

the oils within 20 degrees of each other, around 115°F. You may have to wait a bit for the lye water to cool down. Remember to use a stainless-steel thermometer when measuring it.

When they've reached the right temperatures, pour the oils into a large nonreactive bowl and set it in the sink. Slowly add the lye–water mixture and stir in. Set the plastic spoon in the sink and grab a stainless-steel whisk. Start beating the soap mixture. It may take up to an hour of whisking for the soap to come together, when it reaches a point called trace. Alternatively, you could use an electric immersion blender, in which case you'll only need to beat the mixture for a few minutes.

Either way, you're looking for the soap to thicken enough that a drizzle of the mixture leaves a distinct line on the surface of the soap for a second or two before melting back in, which is the trace point. As soon as you reach trace, stop beating. At this

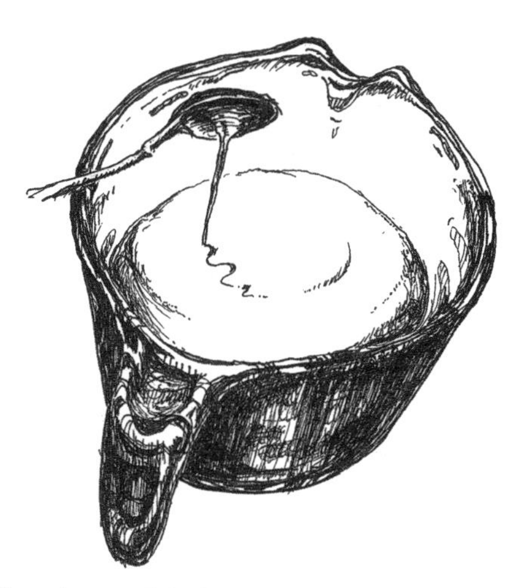

A bit of the mixture drizzled off the spoon will leave a line on the surface. The soap has now reached trace.

point, the soap could thicken rapidly. You can now stir in any essential oils you'd like, up to 1 ounce. Be careful; the soap is still caustic.

Quickly pour the mixture into the prepared soap mold. Cover it, wrap it in a towel, and leave it somewhere relatively warm to cure.

Now go back to your dirty bowls and utensils. Wash off the ones that were in contact with the lye water and either put them back in the recycling or designate them for lye purposes only. The other bowls and utensils are covered in presoap, right? Just put them somewhere safe and out of the way for 24 hours, during which time the soap on them will set up and cease to be caustic. Then you'll simply have dishes covered in soap. What a cinch to clean up.

Meanwhile, the towel-covered soap will start setting up.

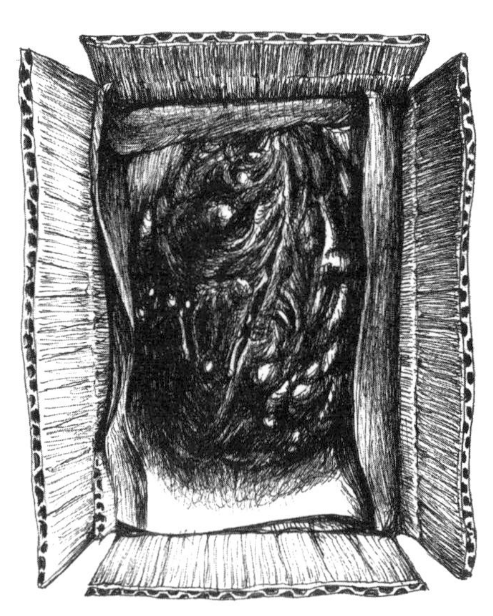

This soap is rising and gelling in the center as it sets up.

Sometimes soap goes through a gel process, during which the saponification generates enough heat that it speeds up its own reaction. The soap will turn translucent in the middle and may even rise and crack. If your soap doesn't gel—and in my experience, hand-whisked soap is less likely to gel—don't worry. Just give the soap 1 or 2 weeks of extra curing time.

After about 48 hours, any self-heating will stop, and the soap will harden. When it's firm enough to cut but still has a slight give, turn it out of the mold and slice it however you like. Set it out on a rack, and put it somewhere warm and airy to cure for 4 weeks (or more, if it didn't gel). After 4 weeks, the soap will be quite hard. Wrap it up and store it away.

Homemade soap does go bad eventually, when the oils go rancid. But it should be fine for up to a year.

Spiced Ghee Soap

Here is a perfect example of the fun you can have coming up with soap recipes. The spices in this recipe turned the soap purple during the gel phase, which surprised and delighted me. Castor oil gives this soap a nice slippery lather, excellent for shaving.

First, make a ghee infusion. Gently melt 3 ounces of ghee and add 10 cloves, 20 or so cardamom pods split open, 10 peppercorns, and a couple of teaspoons of ground cinnamon. Heat it until it smells amazing, then cover it and let the mixture steep for 1 hour or so (or longer).

Strain the ghee infusion through a fine sieve and set it aside. You should have a bit less than 3 ounces. As it sits for a few minutes, the ground cinnamon will settle to the bottom a bit.

Prepare a soap mold and measure 6 ounces of distilled water

and 2⅛ ounces of lye. Stir the lye into the water as described for olive oil soap (page 149), and set it aside to cool.

Melt together 5 ounces of plain ghee, 3 ounces of castor oil, 5 ounces of olive oil, and 1 ounce of coconut oil. Carefully scoop out the top two thirds of the infused ghee (the part with less sediment in it) and add it to the other fats, reserving the bottom third for later.

When the temperature of the oil and lye–water mixture are within 20°F of each other and near 115°F, pour the lye water into the oils and beat as described for olive oil soap until you reach trace.

Add 1 or 2 teaspoons of ground cinnamon to the reserved ghee infusion, and pour it into the soap mixture. Stir a bit, but if you leave it a little swirly, the soap will also be attractively swirly. Pour it into the mold, cover it, and let it cure for 48 hours before unmolding and slicing it. Let the soap dry and harden for another month in a well-ventilated space.

—R

The Epistolary Art

I have always kept a cache of quill pens and a few bottles of ink on my desk. Partly for dramatic effect, but I do use them every now and then to sign a document or doodle. I also do a paleographic workshop in my Tudor and Stuart England class, mostly so students can learn to read Elizabethan secretary hand. The best way to read old scripts is to form the letters yourself. I actually took a whole class in paleography as a grad student, and I've been hooked ever since.

The real beauty of writing with a quill is not necessarily gracefully formed calligraphic strokes. It's how the process slows you down, allows you to reflect on each sentence until properly ripened. It's exactly the opposite of typing on a computer, where words spill out and you correct them later. To begin the epistolary art, you can purchase pens with steel nibs; they'll last a long time and with commercially made ink, you can get going right away. But we like to make things difficult and antiquated. So start with a feather. A goose quill works nicely, but anything will work. The smaller the tip, as with a crow's quill, the thinner the line. My favorite is a pelican feather I found on the beach. With a very sharp penknife cut a diagonal section off the tip of your feather. Then heat up a pan filled with sand and insert the tip into the sand. The idea is to burn out the fibrous insides to create a larger ink chamber. Then carefully split the point down the middle ⅛ to ¼ inch and finally cut the end to a sharp point, keeping the split exactly at the middle if possible.

I know we all imagine a big fluffy feather that billows around with every stroke. This is nonsense and makes writing difficult. Whatever feather you use, trim it to pen size, and trim the

feather fronds, too, so they don't get in your way. Note also, your pen will dull with use; just sharpen it up whenever necessary.

Now to make your ink. Find some oak galls. They are those weird little hard, apple-like growths on oak branches that form when a wasp invades the tree and lays its larvae. Take a handful of these balls, crush them up, and let the crushed galls soak in an old iron pot, or throw in a handful of iron nails, a little rusty is even better. The color comes out only with the addition of iron. After about 1 week boil this mixture until dark and strain through a filter. You will have to add some gum arabic, which can be bought in an art supply shop, to thicken it to writing consistency. Or, as in old days, you can pulverize some dry clean bones into a fine powder. After writing with your ink, dust some of the powder over and blow the rest off. This was standard practice up until about a century ago. Even the Victorian inkwell I keep on my desk has a little shaker for bone powder and two wells for ink.

Now for the writing surface. Paper is okay, but the ink tends to bleed into it and smudge, unless you use a really sturdy stock with high rag content. There is nothing, absolutely nothing, as pleasant as writing on vellum. This is cured, dried, and stretched sheep skin. It's thick and used to be used for official documents, diplomas included, as well as bindings. After working in rare book rooms, you'll soon be able to tell a sixteenth-century book by its light cream-colored vellum binding. Vellum is also not that expensive, about $10 a sheet online. A colleague and I got a whole skin a few years ago, but we still haven't figured out what to do with it; maybe a grimoire.

You can also make your own paper. The easiest way, which is free and great for kids, is to just take an old phone book, soak some shredded pages in water and then pound or whizz them in the blender to make a thick slurry. Pour this out onto an old window screen and soak up the excess water with a sponge, by gently dabbing. Let it dry, then gently remove the paper and put it out in the sun to dry completely. If you don't have a window screen, just staple some nylon screen onto a simple wooden frame, or you can buy a deckle, a kind of frame with chain lines. The rough edge on this kind of paper is called a deckle edge, and people who love this are said to have a deckle fetish. I kid you not. You can drop little flattened dry flowers into the mix, plant parts, grass, anything. Even add food coloring to get varied hues. A little laundry starch in the mix will make the paper smoother as a writing surface. The more difficult way to make paper involves mashing wood pulp, bark, and rags with caustic chemicals, but the method just given is a great way to get started.

As for old paper, I have to say one of the greatest thrills of doing archival research with old manuscripts is not only knowing that someone scrawled out the words five hundred years ago and ogling at the chain lines and watermarks in the paper but occasionally finding a hair that fell from the head of the paper maker into the wet slurry and still remains stuck in the paper. Even more amazing was a farming journal that had weeds stuck into the pages with brass pins, still in place since the 1560s. Frisson! So be sure to take good care of your scribblings, five hundred years from now a historian may be scrutinizing them in some musty archive.

—K

The Simple Broom

I stumbled one day on an edifying little treatise entitled *Broom-Corn and Broom*, published in 1876, written by the editors of the *American Agriculturalist*, a delightful old farming zine. You can find both online. Apparently broom making was a dying art in the nineteenth century, and the editors sought to instruct readers how to grow their own broomcorn (aka sorghum) and make brooms for profit or pleasure. If you're wondering about sorghum, it looks a lot like corn, except that the seeds grow on tassels that shoot up from the top. That's the broom, though other plants have certainly been used as well, including the plant broom in the Genisteae tribe. As for sorghum, the sweet variety is made into syrup, and it's distilled into maotai in China, a potent clear spirit. If you have a little patch, you can grow your own sorghum or buy it. Try R. E. Caddy, a supplier in Greensboro, North Carolina. I know you will find me daft, but I have always found the smell of broom straw exceedingly appetizing.

Here's how to do it. You can make the standard flat broom, good for sweeping, or a rounded besom, which is best for flying around at night and consorting with incubae and succubi. You will need, apart from the broomcorn, a sturdy wooden shaft, such as a branch; some strong hemp twine, preferably of a cheery color; and a stout iron needle; and a table vice if you want a flat broom. There are needles made just for brooms, but a stiff wire with a loop on the end works fine.

First gather the stalks of broom into a bundle, aligning the spot where they begin to branch out. Both ends will then be uneven, but you'll trim them later. Then take a double length of sturdy but thin hemp twine as high as you can reach and tie one end to a hefty stick on the floor. Tie the other end around the broom with a slipknot—the kind that gets tighter as you pull. This is a trick for winding the cord around the broom, as tightly as you can. Just step on the stick with both feet, lift the broom and slowly roll it toward you, so the cord wraps around the stalks tightly. Tie it off with a knot and do it again with another color hemp twine, or three times. If you can, tuck the excess string into the stalks or under the bound strings. Next trim your stalk end evenly with a serrated knife. Then sharpen your handle to a point and ram it directly into the middle of the stalk end of the broom. You can secure the handle with a nail if you like. Trim the sweeping end evenly with a big pair of scissors. You can also

The final stage of making the broom. The bristles are flattened in a vice and stitched with a large needle and hemp thread of diverse colors.

trim the stalk end to taper where it meets the handle. This is the rounded besom, which works perfectly for those tight corners in the kitchen.

If you want a flat sweeping broom, mount a vice on a table and in the part that tightens, put two thin wooden shims and your broom in the middle. Tighten the vice so the broom is flattened and secure. Next you will sew across the broom, once or twice to maintain the flat shape. Basically just sew as you would a hem, keeping in mind it will be visible and decorative, so definitely use colored hemp—green and red are beautiful. It is easiest to grab a little bunch of broom fiber and sew around them twice as you proceed across, just so you aren't breaking off the stalks as you poke your needle through. Not only tidy, but a pleasure to use.

—K

Rings for Weddings or Amusement

When my husband and I decided to get married last year, we spent a while pondering the ring problem. We wanted rings that were significant but not frighteningly expensive, simple but beautiful, and maybe even replaceable. Things get lost, you know. But how in the world can you combine significance with replaceability?

Our solution was to spend a rainy weekend hammering old silver quarters into rings for each other. Should they get lost, we have the skills and tools to just buckle down and make more. In total, the rings cost about $10 apiece, and that was for the tools. They're simple, lovely, and deeply significant.

Of course, you don't have to have serious commitment purposes when making these rings. They say either sailors or prisoners started making coin rings out of boredom, using nothing but spoons to tap them into shape. I learned the method from my father, David Nafziger, who has made many such rings and developed a technique to expedite the process considerably.

Actually, I was prepared for these rings to be a lot more difficult than they were. Once you've gathered all your equipment, you can make a ring in a day. Finding old silver quarters is getting trickier by the year, but you can track them down online or in antique stores. They shouldn't cost more than $5 or so. They stopped making silver quarters in 1965 when the value of the silver exceeded the value of the quarter. Quarters newer than 1964 have copper alloy cores, which will show when you hammer them.

First, you need to measure your ring size. Wrap a slip of paper around your finger at the desired location and mark it where it meets. Measure it in millimeters as carefully as you can. You might even want to repeat the process a few times, at different times of the day. This is the circumference of your finger, so you'll want to divide by π to get the diameter (and no, your finger is not perfectly circular, but the ring will be—so, close enough).

If you have large knuckles, you may also want to note the size of your knuckle, since the ring will have to pass over that. Fortunately, it's quite easy to enlarge a finished ring, but not possible to make it smaller.

Next, you'll need sandpaper in an array of fine grits, a small cylindrical file, and a small hammer—all available at a decent hardware store. You will also want to find something solid and heavy to serve as your anvil. It doesn't need to be very large; I used one of the metal burrs from my grain mill.

You'll also need a long bolt with washers and nuts to hold the quarter in place. The washers and nuts need to be smaller than the finished diameter of the ring—that is, your finger measurement. The bolt gives you something to hang on to when you're hammering. The washers also give the quarter stability, so an errant hammer stroke doesn't fatally warp the coin.

To mount the quarter, drill a hole in the very center large enough to slide over the bolt smoothly. Place washers on either side and secure with the nuts. Now, if you're aiming to make a fairly small ring, note that the smaller the diameter of the ring, the wider the band will be. You can file it down afterward, but if you have access to some equipment, you can take a shortcut here: Mount the quarter on a drill, perfectly centered. Turn it on

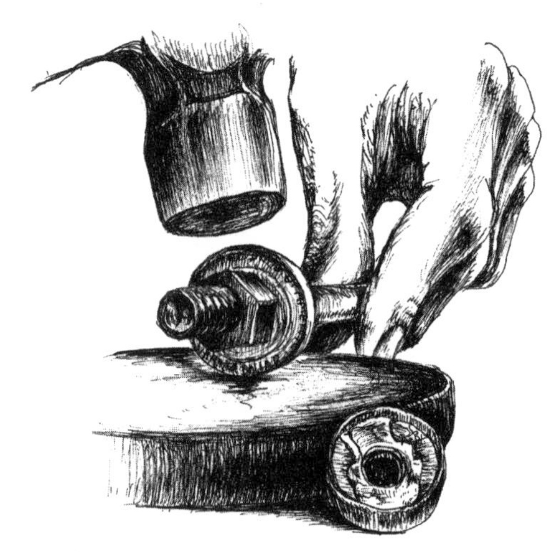

Keep the coin and your hammer strokes vertical to prevent the ring from warping.

so it's whizzing around, then press it evenly against a block of sandpaper or a belt sander to grind off the outer edge of the quarter all the way around. A couple of millimeters is plenty and will save you some hammer time.

Now for the hammering. Place the quarter on the anvil and hold the bolt parallel to the surface so the quarter is vertical. With the hammer, gently tap the edge of the quarter. Take care to keep your strokes straight and centered on the edge of the quarter. Angled strokes will quickly warp the edge. Rotate the quarter every few taps to avoid making flat spots. Keep going. Over the course of hours, the rim of the quarter will widen as it flattens, and the diameter of the quarter will shrink.

As you work, the quarter may get scuffed and blackened, depending on your anvil surface. Don't worry; any grime will quickly disappear in the filing stages.

Once the inside of the quarter reaches the desired width of your ring, you can take it off the bolt. Remember, though, that it's easy to widen a finished ring, but impossible to shrink it. Insert the narrow cylindrical file in the bolt hole and commence widening the hole. Glamorous silver dust will fly!

Then wrap a slightly wider cylinder or spoon handle in medium-grit sandpaper and remove the rest of the quarter's middle right up to the outer band. At that point, you will no longer be able to tell it had once been a quarter.

Check the width of the band. If it's too wide, you can lay it on its side on a piece of sandpaper and grind it down. The flat edge will be a bit sharp; sand it more to round it. Using progressively finer grits of sandpaper, smooth the inside of the ring and finish smoothing the band. The exterior of the band may be slightly dimpled from hammer marks, which you can polish smooth. Or you can leave it as is. Over the years, the ring will wear smoother and smoother.

If you need to enlarge the ring, just slide it over a metal cylinder and gently tap the outside with the hammer. Tap just once or twice before rechecking the size, as subtle differences can dramatically change the fit.

As far as I know, it's only illegal to damage and destroy coins if you plan on reusing them as currency—clearly not the case here.

—R

9

Sewing

When I was first learning how to sew and started showing off a skirt or something I had designed and made, I told someone that sewing was simply the essence of common sense. You just had to stare at your idea from all sides and figure out how to make it exist. In retrospect, I was using the term *common sense* the way many people do, with a certain amount of self-satisfaction, a pinch of false humility. Because, fundamentally, sewing is really engineering, and like an engineer, you have to picture things three dimensionally—you have to flip things over in your head and turn them inside out to see what you're doing. You have to take things apart and put them back together. But you also have to muster all your patience as you pin, and iron, and stitch and stitch and stitch. And then it's design, and it's art, too. You can play with colors like a finger-painting kid and still manage to maintain your image of straitlaced practicality, if that's your thing.

No, sewing is not just common sense, but a commonsense knowledge of how things work is most of what you need to figure it out. I have tried to explain things in this chapter so that you know *why* they work the way they do—to give you a practical understanding of the properties of fabric and fiber, whether you want to design clothing, mend an elbow, or make a quilt.

—R

Grain, Gore, Right, and Wrong: A Handful of Basic Sewing Terms

Grain: A term borrowed from woodworking, grain refers to the direction the fabric's threads are running. Unlike wood, however, woven fabric usually has two grains: the threads running vertically and the threads running horizontally. Most of the time, you can use both grain lines interchangeably, unless the fabric has a directional design (like stripes) or an unusual weave (like a twill).

When you pull a piece of fabric on the grain line, it won't stretch very much. If you pull the fabric on a line diagonal to the grain (on the *bias*), however, it will stretch considerably. This stretchiness, or give, makes a big difference in how clothing fits! For a twill, pick the grain line with the least give as your reference for laying out pattern pieces.

Knit materials are stretchy in every direction, but you still need to pay attention to grain lines—just follow the lines of the knitting.

Right Side/Wrong Side: Printed fabrics and unusual weaves have a wrong side and a right side. If it's not clear which side is supposed to be the right side, pick your favorite and use it consistently.

Seam: A line of stitching joining two pieces of fabric is a seam (see page 168).

Allowance: Extra fabric added to seams and hems to prevent fraying. Usually ½ inch for seams (see page 168) and 3 inches for hems (see page 174).

Hem: The bottom edge of a garment is generally called a hem, but hemming also refers to a particular kind of stitch (commonly used on skirt hems; see page 174).

Basting: Long running stitches used to temporarily hold fabric in place before stitching it (see page 170).

Gore: The truncated-triangle-shaped pieces of fabric used to create the panels in skirts (and umbrellas).

Dart: A tapered tuck used to shape a garment (see page 178).

Useful Tools

You can, in fact, sew with just needle and thread, but a few other tools make it a lot easier.

For starters, it's worth having a wide variety of sewing needles in different thicknesses and lengths. You'll also want sharp sewing scissors to cut fabric without it moving around. You'll need plenty of pins and an iron (see page 176). A seam ripper comes in handy, even if just to remove itchy tags on clothing. You'll sometimes want a yardstick; a tracing wheel and paper can be very helpful for transferring patterns to fabric, but they're not crucial.

And, of course, a functional sewing machine is a fabulous tool. You can sew without one, but there's a very good chance that you can acquire a decent old sewing machine for free or next to nothing, if you're really interested.

Seams

The fundamental principle of sewing: take two pieces of fabric, place right sides together, and line up the raw edges you want to sew. Stitch ½ inch or so from the edge (this distance is the seam allowance).

Some seams are formed in other ways. Topstitching refers to sewing from the top—that is, the *right* side of the cloth, with the material lying flat. Usually you're topstitching a seam you already sewed, to reinforce it. A serged seam is stitched by a special machine, which simultaneously reinforces and trims the raw edge to keep it from fraying.

Less common, a French seam is an enclosed seam with no raw edges showing, even on the inside of the garment. Basically, a French seam is stitched twice: First you stitch wrong sides together halfway between the seam line and the edge. Then you fold the fabric back and stitch right sides together on the intended seam line.

Seam Allowances

Whenever you stitch two pieces of fabric together, you need to allow for extra material, called a seam allowance. Seams need to be well back from the edge of the fabric, or they will fray and rip out. For most cloth, ½ to ⅝ inch is the standard seam allowance. Very coarsely woven or knit cloth (picture burlap and sweaters) requires a large seam allowance, whereas a tight, fine weave might need only ¼ inch. The amount of strain the seam carries also affects the size of the seam allowance. You want a generous seam allowance on a corset, for instance.

Basic Stitches

Sewing machines are excellent devices, but I can't tell you how yours works, and there are always things you'll have to sew by hand. Hand sewing can be a pleasant and efficient process once you catch the rhythm of it. For any given stitch and situation, you should experiment to find the easiest way to hold the fabric and needle. Sometimes just changing the orientation of the fabric can make it much easier to stitch. Right to left? Up to down? When you're comfortable and get into a rhythm, your stitches become much more even and regular.

To avoid tangles and frustration, cut your thread no longer than an arm's length (or two arms' lengths, if you're doubling it). For shorter work, cut your thread about three times the length of the finished seam, or twice the length for a basic running stitch.

Securing the Thread

On fine, tightly woven fabrics, a knot in your thread will secure it on the underside of the fabric. On looser fabrics, a loop is more secure. I often sew with doubled thread. Load a thread through your needle, then hold both ends of the thread together and tie them in a knot. Make your first stitch as usual, then when the needle comes back to the underside of the fabric, slip it through the loop formed by the two knotted threads. This is a very secure anchor.

When you're done stitching and ready to tie off your thread, poke the needle through to the underside and slide it under your last stitch. Twist the needle around the thread right where it came through the fabric and pull to form a knot.

Running Stitch

The running stitch is the basic up-and-down stitch: Poke the needle down through the fabric, then poke it back up a little farther along. Because the stitches all go one direction, the fabric can bunch up and slide along the thread when it's pulled taut. Running stitches don't make a secure seam, but they're useful if forming gathers is your purpose. They're also quite quick to make—you can load several stitches on your needle before you pull the thread through.

Sometimes when you're sewing a particularly tricky spot, pins won't hold the fabric securely enough for you to sew it properly—or maybe you want to make a quick temporary seam and check how the garment fits before committing to a real seam. In these cases, running stitches spaced ¼ inch apart can hold the fabric together for a bit and then be undone quite easily. This is called basting.

Running stitches are also used for quilting, once the layers of the quilt are assembled and tacked in place. With multiple thicknesses of cloth, puckering and gathering are less of a worry.

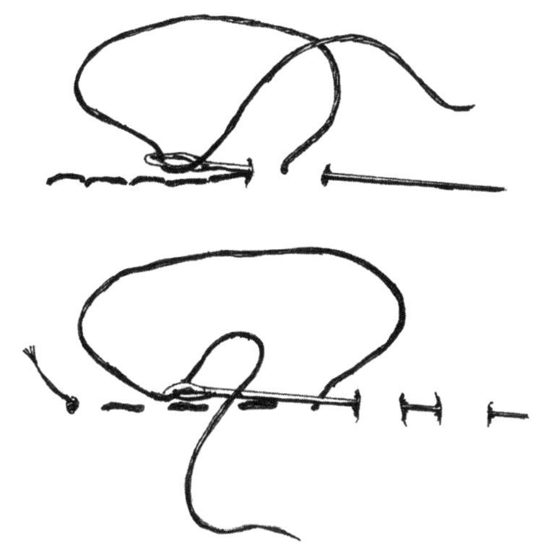

The basic embroidery stitch (top) backtracks to form a secure, solid line. Running stitch, bottom.

Backstitch

The backstitch solves the gathering problem of the running stitch by going one step back, then two steps forward. Secure the thread on the underside of the fabric, then bring the thread up through. Poke the needle down through the cloth ⅛ inch in the opposite direction from where you want to go, then bring it back up ⅛ inch ahead of the starting point. For each backstitch after the first, you can poke the needle down through the same hole as the previous stitch, or right beside it. The finished product will look like a continuous line of end-to-end stitches. The underside of the fabric will look a little messier, with stitches leapfrogging each other.

You can, of course, modify this stitch in any number of ways. The ⅛-inch spacing is certainly adjustable, and the stitches don't have to meet each other. The inverse stitch, done carefully, forms a line that looks like a twisted rope—in embroidery, it's called the stem stitch.

Even with the backstitch, you must be careful to build in a little flex. Pulled perfectly taut, the backstitch will bind the fabric more than the average machine stitch. Hold the fabric taut in your hand as you're working or put it in an embroidery hoop. If your fabric is slacker than your stitches, the stitches will bind it and the seam won't lie smooth.

Whipstitch

The whipstitch is especially useful when a straight row of backstitches would be too binding. It's easy and quick, and you'll need it for hems, attaching patches, and stitching seams you can access only from the outside. Sewn with bold thread, it has a decorative charm that manufacturers try to emulate whenever they want something to look adorably handsewn.

Secure the thread and pull it up through the fabric at a spot ⅛ inch below the edge of the fabric. Pull it up through the fabric again, this time ⅛ inch to the side of the spot you brought it through before. Repeat.

If your fabric doesn't have an edge, you'll have to poke it down through the fabric at an imaginary edge line. If you poke it through the fabric directly above the spot where your stitch came out, you'll wind up with a row of neat little vertical stitches with angled stitches on the reverse side of the fabric (basically an inverse hemstitch).

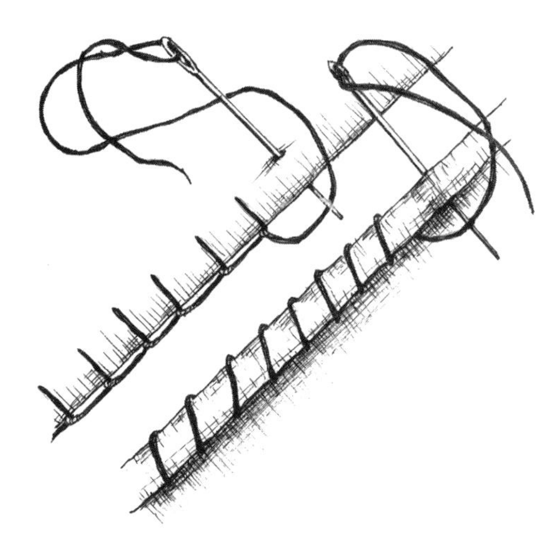

Blanket stitch on the left, whipstitch on the right.

Blanket Stitch

The blanket stitch is a modified whipstitch. It looks great as a finishing stitch on the edges of blankets, of course, but by varying the distance between stitches and the stitch lengths themselves, you can create patterns fancy enough for the edges of silk handkerchiefs, too. Because *obviously* you have dozens of silk handkerchiefs languishing for want of embellishment.

I like to start with the edge of the fabric down. Secure the thread on the underside and pull it up through ¼ inch above the edge. Make the next stitch by pulling the needle up through a spot ¼ inch to the side of the previous spot. This time, be sure your needle passes *over* the thread as in the illustration above. Tug it gently into place and repeat.

The very first stitch will be a bit slanted, but the others will be nice and square. If you're sewing a blanket, you can leave the first stitch slightly slack and catch it in the final stitch when you come all the way back around.

Hems

Hemming is a preeminently useful skill, since it's necessary for lengthening and shortening ready-made clothes as well as constructing new ones. It's also a frequently demanded repair. Hemstitching is not just for the bottoms of clothes, either—it's useful on sleeves, curtains, and tablecloths, too.

You need to leave *at least* a couple of inches for a hem. A very small hem allowance creates awkward stiffness in the hem owing to the tightly folded fabric, which braces the material. The heavier the fabric, the more hem allowance you should leave. Extra material in the hem will also give you leeway should you wish to lengthen the garment later.

Seams bind and tighten the fabric on which they're sewn, preventing the weave from shifting and stretching slightly in the direction of the seam. Usually this is a good thing, but not in the case of hems. An ordinary seam on the edge of the fabric will cause it to stiffen and pucker, so it doesn't drape smoothly.

Thus hemstitching is loose—the individual stitches are about ⅜ inch apart—and the stitches themselves are perpendicular to the hem. This way they don't line up and bind the fabric. Hemstitches don't bear a lot of weight or strain, so they can get away with being delicate.

Good hemstitches are also invisible. When the needle dips down to the outside of the garment, it only catches a thread or two before coming back to the wrong side. A tiny pucker, eased with ironing, should be all that's visible.

First, determine where you'd like the edge of the garment to be. Try it on inside out and have some help pinning up the raw edge of the fabric so the bottom is level with the floor (or properly angled if that's what you're after) at the desired height. Pinning can be a little bit tricky on the hem of an A-line skirt, since the raw bottom edge will be wider than the part you're pinning it to. Try to keep the excess evenly distributed, and pin frequently.

You now have a folded edge on the bottom of your garment. If you're working on a full A-line skirt, it might help you to iron the pinned fold now to keep the evenly distributed excess fabric in place.

Next, fold under the raw edge about ½ inch, and pin it in place. Choose a thread that closely matches the material. Anchor the thread to the inside fabric and make a tiny downward stitch, dipping the needle under just a few threads of the exterior fabric before coming back up through the folded-down edge of the

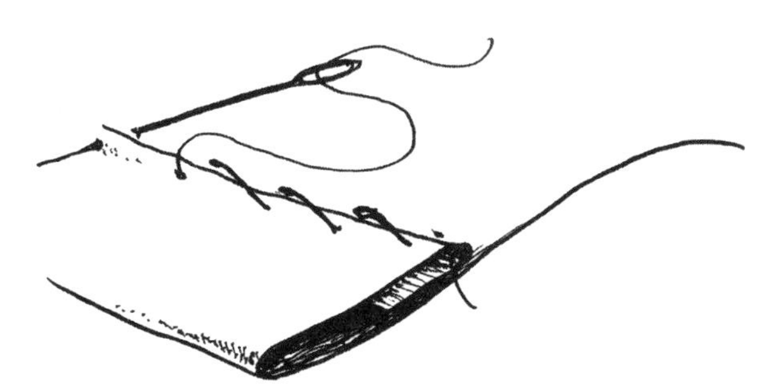

When stitching a hem, the tiny vertical stitches should be barely visible on the reverse side.

inside fabric. You're basically making a whipstitch that barely snags the outside of the garment.

After stitching the entire hem, iron it carefully. Use steam on cotton or wool to relax the fibers and ease any excess material into place.

On Pins and Irons

The fact of the matter is, most of sewing is planning and engineering. The rest of it is pinning and ironing, with a tiny bit of actual stitching thrown in. First you must pin your pattern pieces before you can cut them. Then you must pin your fabric pieces together before you can stitch them. You pin when you're fitting, when you're hemming, and when you're mending. If you're really an A student, you might even baste everything you pin, and then sew it again for real.

The point of all these pins is to keep the fabric from sliding around. You start stitching together two equally long pieces of fabric and by the time you reach the end of the seam they will not—I guarantee you—still match up, unless you've pinned them at reasonable intervals. A reasonable pinning interval is a few inches for straight, flat seams parallel to the grain. If the fabric is cut at an angle to the grain (aka on the bias) or if you're negotiating seam intersections (darts, gathers, sleeves, or other interesting topography), you might have to pin every ½ inch or less, and probably baste, too.

Sometimes, even then, you might find yourself dealing with a heavy wool material of an unusual weave that stretches more in some directions than in others and at least one edge of every gore in the skirt is on the bias, and no matter how you pin, the skirt pieces will not match up. That's why you leave a very generous hem allowance, especially on your wedding dress.

Ironing is the other side of pinning. You should iron your material before you lay out the pattern pieces, and later, your seams will not lie smooth until they have been ironed open.

To press open a seam, lay it flat on the ironing board with the raw side facing up. With your fingers, separate the two raw edges and fold them back in opposite directions (like opening a book). Come behind with the iron, smoothing them into place.

Occasionally it is necessary to press *both* raw edges together onto one side of the seam—for narrow darts, for example. But most of the time, even when the finished garment will be folded on the seam, you still want to press the seam open first.

Buttons

Because it's easier to move a button than a buttonhole, you should sew your buttonholes first. Cut a slit in your material large enough for the button to pass through, erring on the small side (at first). Seal up the raw edge of the slit with very tight, close whipstitches. When you're almost all the way around, check the button again. The whipstitching can change the way the hole fits over the button. Adjust the size of the buttonhole now, if you need to, then finish whipstitching.

When sewing on a button, use double thread and anchor it solidly. Stitch through the loops or the buttonholes more times than you think necessary—dozens of times, at least. Be aware that your stitches can gradually shift the button's position as you're working, so check regularly to make sure the button is staying centered on the spot it's supposed to be.

If you're designing something from scratch, remember to leave extra material for the button overlap—and even more if you want to double the fabric back to make a sturdy button placket.

Darts and Tucks

The tricky thing about darts and tucks is that they turn flat fabric pieces into three-dimensional surfaces. That, of course, is why they're so useful! But it also means that getting them to look smooth and flat is a bit of a chore because, in fact, they *aren't* flat.

Take darts. First, transfer or draw the dart lines onto the inside of the fabric—it should look like an isosceles triangle with a line bisecting it. Your job is to stitch together the sides of the

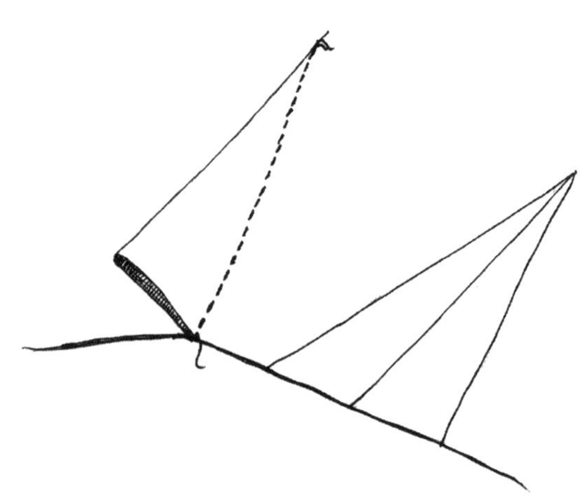

To form a dart, fold the fabric on the center line (dotted) and stitch the solid lines together.

triangle. Fold the cloth on the midline so the midline forms a ridge (not a valley). If you had X-ray vision, you could see that the other two lines match up perfectly. Pin the cloth in place and stitch along the line. Be especially careful at the point of the dart. Any veering or puckering will be very noticeable when the fabric is opened up.

If the dart is more than 1½ inches at the base, you may want to trim it parallel to the seam, leaving ½ inch of seam allowance. Otherwise, press the dart to one side or the other. Most darts come in pairs, so be sure to press them in symmetrical directions. Pressing will be rather tricky at this stage, since the material is no longer flat. Try pressing it over the narrow end of the ironing board or the end of a table.

There is another type of dart that is shaped like a diamond. It's essentially two darts stacked and shows up in waistlines.

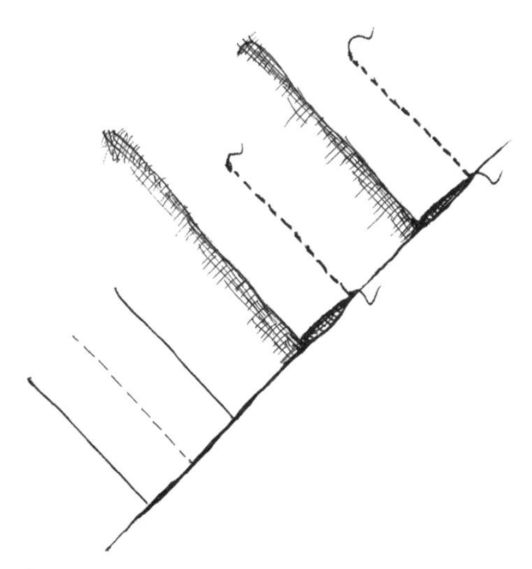

To form a tuck, fold the fabric on the dotted line and stitch the solid lines together.

Tucks are a bit easier because they have no point to contend with. When pressing them, take care not to press the fold beyond the end of the stitching, unless pleats are your intention.

Embroidery

Most of the basic hand-sewing stitches are easily adapted to decorative purposes. Use embroidery floss or fine yarn to give your labor some emphasis. Mark your designs directly on the fabric with light pencil first, or just freehand doodle with your needle. It's a good idea to practice new designs on scrap cloth first to get the feel of them.

Since embroidery floss is composed of multiple tiny threads only loosely held together, tangles and knots form easily and are immensely frustrating. Save yourself some trouble: Cut your thread on the short side and use a needle with a large eye.

An embroidery hoop holds the fabric taut for you, which makes it easier to get precise results on tightly woven fabric. Move the hoop around to keep the area you're working on in the center of the hoop. Embroidery hoops are useless for stretchy material (and yes, you can embroider stretchy material—it will just stretch less and/or pucker in the embroidered areas).

I'll quickly describe a handful of fun embroidery stitches, but you're free to invent your own. To make a chain stitch, for instance, bring the needle up through the material and back down through the same spot or very near, leaving a loop of thread. Bring the needle back up through the material at the spot where you want the next link in the chain. Hook the needle through the loop, and poke it back down where it just came up, once gain leaving a loop to catch in the next stitch. Gently tug everything into place. Repeat.

To make a flower petal or leaf, start making a chain stitch, but don't make a second loop. Just catch the first loop and poke the needle back down to tack the loop in place. If you form a chain stitch but don't poke the needle down right next to where it comes out, you'll make a branching fernlike stitch.

You can fill in larger color blocks with a satin stitch. These are just large parallel stitches that traverse the area from one edge to the other, laid down side by side to fill in a space. If the stitches get too long and start sagging and looking bad, you can weave a few perpendicular stitches across the satin stitches to hold them in place.

The stem stitch (an inverse backstitch) and the chain stitch are useful not just for drawing lines but also for filling in larger areas.

Alterations

One of the easiest and most gratifying ways to create unique and stylish garments is to start with something much less unique and stylish, and modify it. Conveniently, it's also more economical than purchasing new fabric by the yard. Knowing how to alter clothing for fit also expands your options significantly.

Width

You can easily fix a skirt waistband that rides too high or low, provided you renegotiate any zippers. Determine the new size you'd like the waistband to be, and where it will fall on your waist. With a seam ripper, pick out the stitches attaching the waistband to the skirt.

To narrow the waistband, sew a tuck of the appropriate size into the back middle of the band. Then, you have several choices for how to narrow the skirt itself. You can either sew a pair of darts or tucks into the back of the skirt, or take in the preexisting seams. The total width of the darts or tucks should be the same as the width of the waistband tuck. Sew the waistband back on.

To lengthen the waistband, you will probably need to add some material. Either find a scrap of similar material, and stitch that onto the end of the old waistband (or into the middle, for symmetry), or construct a new waistband from scratch. The skirt itself will need to be trimmed to fit the new waistband. Since skirts usually widen as they descend from the waistband toward the hip, you need to locate the point where the skirt reaches your desired width, mark it, and then trim off the top ½ inch or so above that point. Be cautious here. Even a tiny amount of trimming can dramatically widen the waist opening of the skirt, depending on its cut. In any case, the skirt will slacken and sag when you trim it as its lengthwise seams unravel slightly, but reattaching the waistband will restore its structure.

Pants are significantly more difficult to alter in the widthwise dimension because they can't simply be adjusted up or down on the body like skirts. In most cases, however, they can be taken in by tucking the waistband and taking in the side seams, as described for skirts. There is usually not enough excess material to let them out. You could certainly take apart the side seams and insert strips of material, preferably colorful tie-dyed fabric from a Grateful Dead tapestry.

It's not difficult to take in the legs of a pair of pants to create skinny jeans. Put the pants on inside out and determine how much to take them in and where. Pin them while they're on you, so you can check to make sure you can still get your feet out of the bottom. Take them off and mark the places where the new seams should go. Taper them gradually, or you'll get a knicker-like effect. If you can, take in only one seam on each leg: The seam that isn't topstitched or the seam on the side of the leg with the most flare (in both cases, that's usually the outside seam). If you're taking in a lot of material, you may want to take in both leg seams. Stitch the new seam on the marked lines, then rip out the old seam. Press the seam open. You may need to undo the hem and rehem it for a clean, finished look (on denim, this is usually just a topstitched rolled hem, so not a big deal).

To narrow shirts and blouses, take in the side seams or add darts. Do so with some caution, however, or the shoulders may wind up looking out of balance and bunchy when the shirt no longer has so much fullness and drape. Taking in the shoulders is a bit of a trick because it involves taking off the sleeves.

Length

Shortening pants, skirts, or sleeves is usually fairly easy. In most cases, you can simply undo the current hem, fold the fabric up farther, and rehem it.

Sleeves with cuffs are slightly more tricky. First, note how the tucks or gathers are distributed. Remove the cuff and either trim the sleeve or just slide the cuff farther up over the end of the sleeve. Then pin the cuff back on, being careful to distribute the tucks or gathers as they were before. Topstitch the cuff in place.

To lengthen cuffed sleeves, feel how much seam allowance is on the end of the sleeve inside the cuff. You can maybe lengthen the sleeve a bit by turning a ½-inch sleeve allowance into a ¼-inch sleeve allowance, but sturdiness may be sacrificed. At least reinforce the raw edge of the fabric with zigzag stitching, but that only goes so far.

To lengthen pants or a skirt (or hemmed or lined sleeves), you'll need to check that there is enough excess material built into the hem. You might be able to eke out a little more length by using hem tape. Stitch the edge of the fabric to the hem tape, and then hemstitch the hem tape.

Mending

Many holes in garments aren't holes in the fabric, but rather places where the stitching has ripped out. These sorts of holes are the easiest and least obtrusive mending jobs. If the garment isn't lined, you can just turn it inside out, fold it at the seam, and stitch along the existing stitching line over the ripped-out section. Be sure to overlap the intact stitches by 1 inch or so on either side. You can do this even on serged or French seams. If you follow the old stitching line exactly, use matching thread, and don't make the stitches so tight that the fabric puckers, your mending will be perfectly invisible.

If you can only access the seam from the outside of the garment, you can still make a tidy, nearly invisible repair. For a small hole, 1 to 2 inches, make little running stitches on the seam lines back and forth across the hole. Be sure that each stitch is passing through only one layer of the material. Pulled taut (but not puckering), these stitches will be invisible. Anchor the thread 1 inch from the torn spot on either side.

For a larger hole, you'd be wise to pin the edges together, to avoid stitching the seam crookedly. You'll also want to use a backstitch, to prevent the fabric from gathering and puckering.

Patching

There are two basic ways to patch a hole: from the inside, and from the outside. Small holes with some threads still connected can be unobtrusively patched from the inside. Larger, messy holes are better patched from the outside, so they don't snag and reopen. You can, of course, put a patch on both sides, to prevent snagging on both sides of the cloth, but then you must start to worry about the weight of the patch itself straining the original material.

In fact, being able to decide whether a patch is worthwhile is one of the key skills of patching. The chafing edges of the patch and the extra stitches themselves put an additional strain on already-worn material. That said, patching usually takes just a few minutes and can extend the life of a pair of work jeans for months or years, definitely a worthwhile attempt. You can also apply a preemptive patch. My mother used to do this for the knees of all our sweat pants, and the trend is well established on the elbows of professorial jackets.

Consider the original material quite closely. If it's becoming brittle or all-over thread-worn, you might wind up with more patch than original garment, which isn't necessarily a reason to give up hope, depending on your aesthetics. Be particularly wary of patching stretch denim, as once it starts to wear out, it goes downhill quickly. Delicate fabrics will no longer drape the same way once they are patched, but with some care, you can minimize the effect. Loose-knit fabrics, like sweaters, are often best patched with matching yarn woven across the hole (darning).

You will want to find a patching material that matches the original in terms of thickness, weight, stiffness, and stretch. A heavy patch will cause the garment to pucker or stick out oddly, or tug the threads out of their weave. A thin patch will wear out more quickly than the original material.

Your stitches themselves should also match the fabric type. Even on tightly woven fabric, try to avoid tight straight lines of stitches, as they will bind the fabric, making the patch not only uncomfortable but also more likely to rip out. Instead, use whipstitches or zigzag stitches to build in some flex.

INTERIOR PATCH

An interior patch is an excellent way to mend the tiny holes formed at the upper corners of your back pockets (just don't stitch through the pocket itself), moth holes, or small rips from barbed wire and brambles.

Cut your patching material to be 2 inches larger than the hole in all directions. You can trim it down later. Keeping the garment right-side out, slide the patch up inside behind the hole, and pin it in place. With either a machine or by hand, run stitches around the outside of the hole (on good cloth, not the frayed edges). Then trim the loose edges and tack them down with zigzag or whipstitches. It wouldn't hurt to put another row of reinforcing stitches ½ inch from the edge of the hole, if there's a good deal of tension and friction in that area.

Now turn the garment inside out and trim the edges of the patch, leaving a ½ inch of fabric beyond the outer stitches.

EXTERIOR PATCH

The exterior patch is almost like an inverse of the interior patch, except that appearances are more important. Before stitching on the patch, you will want to fold the edges under ½ inch or so to avoid raw fraying edges on the outside—this means you need to cut your patch size to be at least ½ inch larger than the hole, plus ½ inch extra to fold down.

You might also want to avoid stitching the fraying edges of the hole directly to the patch, if the idea of extra stitching lines on the patch is bothersome to you. Instead, you'll want to reinforce the edges of the hole before covering it with the patch. Trim away the loose threads and run zigzag or whipstitches first around the very edge of the hole and then ¼ inch from the edge. Position the patch, pin it, and stitch it down at the edges. Put in another row of stitches, this time ¼ inch from the edges.

For the greatest security, and if you don't mind how it looks, pin and stitch the patch over the hole as described, then turn the garment inside out and stitch all the fraying edges directly onto the patch, leaving as many of the fraying threads intact as you can without them being annoying and snaggy. Put in a generous amount of reinforcement stitching ¼ inch and ½ inch from the edge of the hole.

Darning

Large, open knit garments, like sweaters, are vulnerable not so much to fraying as unraveling. So mending them requires you to take a different tack: darning, which is essentially a weaving process. You can also darn certain types of holes in denim—like the knee holes that still have lots of horizontal threads crossing them.

Choose yarn the same thickness as the garment's yarn. With a large blunt needle, start laying down the warp threads, keeping the stitches a safe distance (½ inch, or less for tighter knits) away from the hole. The stitches should be slightly loose—not baggy, but far from tight. If they are too tight, they will simply unravel the sweater further.

When you have covered the hole entirely with warp threads, plus ½ inch on each side, you can start laying down the weft. These stitches are just like the warp stitches, except you have to weave them under and over every other warp thread. For each weft stitch, go under the warp threads you went over on the last stitch, and vice-versa. When you've completely woven across the warp threads, push the needle through to the wrong side of the garment and anchor the end by tying a little knot onto a loop in the sweater.

When darning the heel of a sock or the elbow of a sleeve, it can be helpful to push a light bulb inside to give you something to work against. The light bulb also ensures that the darned hole will curve out like the heel of a sock is supposed to.

Decorative Modifications: Pleats, Ruffles, and Other Trim

I once found an adorable 1960s corduroy minidress at Goodwill. The dress fit perfectly, but the stiff, A-line, super-short skirt was just too big a liability. I found a nice contrasting corduroy material and made a heavy full pleat, which I stitched to the bottom of the dress. The dress, now at a comfortable length, also gained some amazing saucy swish *and* the weight of the trim improved the way the entire dress draped.

Another time, I found a 1970s wrap dress made of gauzy layers. The bodice was an atrocious, unflattering pile of ruffles. I cut it off and stitched a waistband on to the skirt, which actually had a stylish two-layer hem. The layeredness, however, needed a little more definition, so I embroidered both layers of the hem with thick black thread. (In fact, I invented a special sort of knotted, twisted blanket stitch, which I have since forgotten how to do!)

Then there were the sleeves on my wedding dress. (Sleeves on a wedding dress?! If you're getting married on the coast of Oregon, yes!) The heavy wool material just didn't hang right. On a whim, I grabbed some leftover pleat trim and pinned it onto the sleeves. Instantly they looked finished and draped just right.

The point is that trim plays two roles. It can visually transform a garment, but it also builds weight into the fabric, which becomes momentum when you move. And momentum is swishing, draping, swirling—fun things to have in your toolbox, whether you're designing something from scratch or modifying another garment.

Ruffles are an obvious choice, and they don't necessarily have to be gingham bits of country charm on the hem of your skirt. Ruffles exaggerate the stiffness of your material; soft fabrics make less puffy ruffles. You can either hem a ruffle, fold it double, or (on delicate fabrics) give it a tiny rolled hem.

Cut a strip of fabric as wide as you want the finished ruffle to be, plus seam allowance on one side and hem allowance on the other. It needs to be one-and-a-half to three times as long as the fabric edge you're attaching it to—the longer it is, the more folded and fluffy the ruffle will be. If it's too short, it won't look like a ruffle, just a badly sewn strip of fabric that didn't really match up right. You might have to sew a few strips together to be long enough.

To gather the ruffle, baste it with loose running stitches (½ inch) ¼ or ⅛ inch from the raw edge. If you're stitching a long ruffle, it might be easier to baste and gather the ruffle in sections. Pull on the ends of the thread until the fabric bunches up to the right length. Spread the gathers out evenly, pin in place, and sew. Topstitching also works well on ruffles. In either case, don't bother pressing the seam open; just press it away from the ruffle.

Pleating is basically controlled gathering. The fullest a pleat can reasonably be is three times the length of the material you're stitching it to. Prepare your material as for gathering, above. Decide where you want the folds to fall, and mark those points on the fabric. Then go along the strip, folding and pinning where you marked it. Attach the pleat to the material and pin in place. For heavy material, I recommend topstitching the pleat rather than treating it like an ordinary seam. Just as for a ruffle, don't press the seam open; press it away from the pleat.

Other sorts of decorative trim (such as ribbon, braid, and lace) are usually topstitched to the outside of the garment or tacked invisibly to the underside of hems, necklines, and sleeves, where they can peek out.

Clothing Design

The real thrill in sewing is inventing things, and then wearing them. Sewing from store-bought patterns is useful as an exercise, but such clothes will neither fit like custom clothing nor reveal the full powers of your imagination.

It's true that store-bought patterns assume you will modify them to fit your figure, but fitting can be pretty confusing without some knowledge of how patterns are developed in the first place. And if you neglect fitting, you're left with clothes that either hang sack-style or rely on elastic for their structure (and all the bunching that goes along with elastic). Sewing patterns are particularly prone to these faults because the designers know you can't try on a sewing project before you've actually gone to the trouble of making it, so they err on the side of excess material.

I'm going to focus here on dress design simply because designing a dress involves most of the problems you'll face when designing things generally. The bodice of the dress is particularly troublesome. You know how hard it is to make a flat map of a round earth? Ha. Spheres are *easy*. They are so predictable. Mapping a body is the real challenge—creating a three-dimensional surface with two-dimensional cloth. The neat linear progression of clothing sizes obscures the great variety of body shapes and isn't actually either neat or linear when it comes to women's clothing.

You have a distinct advantage over manufacturers in that you need concern yourself with only your own body (or whomever you're making clothing for), and not averages of millions of people or fashion model ideals.

As with many things, the key to design success is starting with a draft. If you will be making a lot of clothes, it's worth the trouble to make yourself a sloper. A sloper is basically a dress model laid flat—it's the clothing-pattern version of you, a second skin made of fabric. You can use it to modify any pattern you have found and modify it to generate patterns that will be sure to fit right.

> To make a sloper, start with a generic fitted bodice pattern approximately your size. Cut it out in a cheap but tightly woven cloth like muslin (or a reasonably firm old sheet), stitch it together, and try it on. Adjust the fit with pins, tucking it along the seams or preexisting dart lines or marking places where it needs to be let out, until you have a close fit, without pulling, bunching, or sagging. It should fit closer than most clothes—when you go to make a clothing pattern from it, you'll add the necessary ease to make it comfortable. Take it off and stitch it along the new lines. Try it on again and iterate the process until you have a perfect fit. Mark the final seam and dart lines, take the garment apart, and lay it out flat. Cut the pattern along the marked lines (don't worry about seam allowances now), and then trace each piece onto cardboard. This collection of cardboard pattern pieces is a two-dimensional representation of your body and is incredibly useful.
>
> Have a new pattern you want to try? Lay the sloper pieces over it to see what adjustments you'll need to make. The style of the

dress will dictate how much ease to allow for, but in the horizontal dimension, the difference between the sloper and the pattern should be consistent. Don't worry if the pattern's darts don't fall in the same location as the sloper's—just be sure that the cumulative width of the darts matches.

To use the sloper to create a pattern, trace it onto paper, add ease and seam allowances, and whatever peculiar design features you have in mind. Darts can move around, so long as they point at generally the same spot and their total width remains constant. Or darts can turn into princess seams, tucks, pleats, or gathers.

If you just want to jump into a particular project, you can combine the fitting stage and the design into one project: the muslin. A *muslin* is a cheap mockup of a pattern, made to be brutally altered and experimented with. In order to get an accurate representation of fit and drape, it's important that you use material fairly similar to what you'll use in your final product, in terms of weight and stretch.

Now, for your pattern. You've filled sketchbooks with ideas for how this dress should look. You want it to have a wide, fitted waistband, say, and princess seams, and a slightly rounded square neckline. Or maybe you want mega-puffy sleeves and a dropped V-shaped waistline. Maybe you want a dress just like the moth-eaten purple one you found in an abandoned house. Between articles of clothing that you already own, and patterns you can browse in a sewing store, and the vast Internet, you can figure out the general shape and size of the pattern pieces you'll need. As for the specifics, some of them are in your head, and some of them will show up only after the tenth iteration of the fitting process. This is why you make a muslin!

Bodice

If you don't have a sloper ready at hand, I recommend scouring the thrift store for a dress with a bodice similar to the one you have in mind, that fits you fairly well, and that you don't love for its own sake. Avoid knits, or anything with stretch (unless your finished dress will be stretchy, in which case you'd better find something with the same amount and type of stretch as your finished dress). You want a firm, tight weave to get an accurate template. The skirt and sleeves don't matter so much, as you can easily swap them out for other designs.

I'm very much in favor of taking things apart to find out how they're made. You can certainly trace pattern pieces from preexisting clothing, but it's quite tricky to get an accurate tracing without taking the dress apart. Especially if there's a lot of tailoring in the form of darts, pleats, tucks, and gathers (and if there isn't—what's the point? Go trace a flour sack).

Pick out the stitches and rip the seams of this dress to give yourself a quick starting point for your pattern. How much seam allowance do the pieces have? It's most accurate to ignore the manufacturer's seam allowances—many manufactured seams are serged, which means your seam allowance will need to be greater than theirs. In addition, some seams may be worn and fraying. It's easiest to just fold the seam allowance out of the way or cut it off (if you're not interested in sewing the garment back together). You'll add your own seam allowance later. In any case, it's a good idea to iron the fabric pieces smooth before tracing

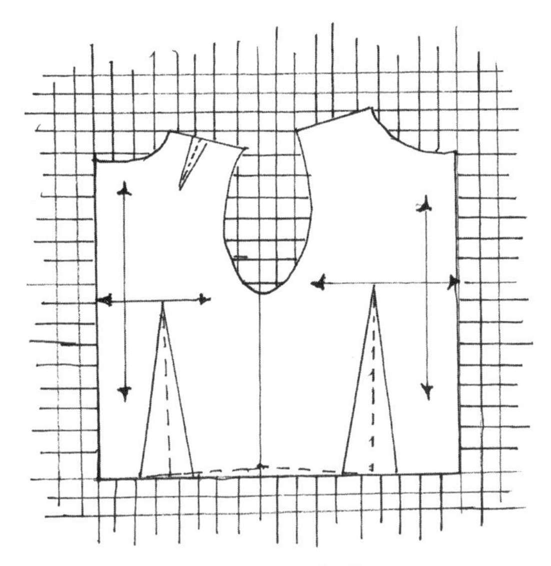

The general shape of a bodice pattern.

them. Lay them out on paper, taking care not to stretch or distort them, and trace them carefully. Then draw a line on the pattern pieces to indicate the grain of the cloth and mark any useful points of reference (buttons, dart lines, etc.).

Make your creative modifications and add seam allowances to the traced paper pieces, and then lay them out on your muslin, lining them up with the grain of the fabric, of course. Pin them securely; cut them out; stitch any darts, tucks, or gathers; and start stitching the pieces together. You can deal with sleeves and skirts later; for now you just want the bodice to fit right. When you try it on, be aware that the weight of the skirt will certainly affect how the bodice hangs, but you'll have to use your imagination for now. Also, any raw edges at the neckline, hem, or other openings will stretch more than they will in the finished product. It wouldn't hurt to run a line of stitching around these areas so they have less give. Pay attention to the fit of the armholes, too; other adjustments you make can change the size of the openings.

The fitting and adjusting process requires a lot of patience. Be sure that *every* time you modify the muslin, you make the corresponding modification to your paper patterns.

Note: You can always use the finished, adjusted muslin as the lining for your dress, provided you sew it inside out. This will only matter if there are asymmetrical pieces (like for buttons, where one side of the dress overlaps the other).

A WORD ON SLEEVES

Once the bodice is complete, you can attach your sleeves. If you have never attached sleeves before, take a deep breath and get plenty of pins handy. When adjusting the bodice, did you make any changes that would affect the size of the arm opening? the arm opening changes whenever you take in or let out the side seams, shoulder seams, princess seams, or darts that open onto the armhole (aka armscye).

Presumably, if the bodice is done, your arm still fits comfortably through the armhole, but now you'll need to adjust the sleeve pattern. With a cloth measuring tape, carefully measure around the armholes in the finished bodice. Next, carefully measure your existing sleeve pattern between the seam allowances, making sure to bend it precisely around all the curves (use pins to prop it in place as you go). Puffy sleeves will always be significantly larger than the opening, but all sleeves should be at least ½ to 1 inch larger; this is the ease allowance.

First, mark the top point of the sleeve curve. Stitch the

sleeve to itself lengthwise and hem it. To attach the sleeve, turn the bodice and the sleeve inside out, and slide the sleeve into the armscye. Pin the sleeve seam to the underarm seam, and the marked spot to the shoulder seam. Pin the rest of the sleeve carefully. Since the sleeve fabric is longer than the sleeve opening, you'll have to ease them together, distributing the excess fabric carefully. If the sleeve is puffy, keep most of the excess fabric to the top of the sleeve (and a very puffy sleeve will warrant a preliminary basting stitch to gather it before attachment). For a smooth sleeve, distribute the excess evenly so no actual folds form. You'll be pinning at least every ½ inch.

Stitch in place with your usual seam allowance. Don't press the seam open; press the seam together away from the bodice.

Skirts

You can fairly easily conjure a simple skirt pattern from thin air, after carefully examining some samples. Pencil and A-line skirts have roughly rectangular and triangular gores, respectively. Gathered skirts can be made of large rectangular (or triangular) pieces, but they generally require fabric be one-and-a-half to three times the desired finished width.

PENCIL SKIRT

Measure your waist at the point the skirt will hang from (the bottom of the bodice, if it's part of a dress). Measure the widest part of your hips, as this will determine the width of the panels you need to cut. Then decide how long you'd like the skirt to be and how many gores you'd like (two or four are common). Pencil

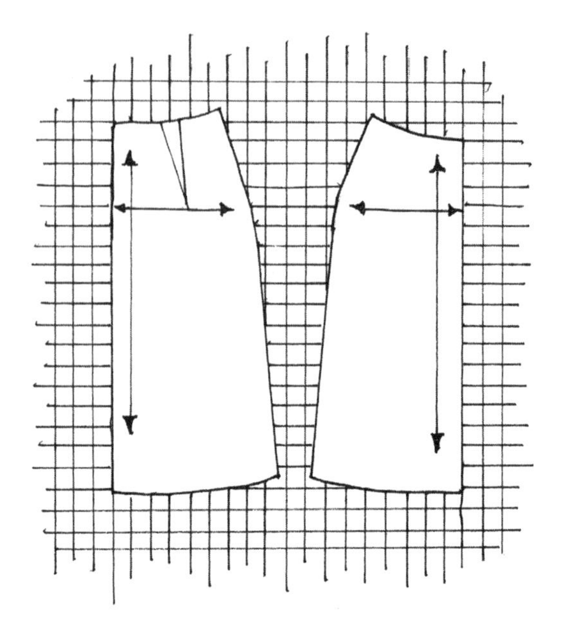

A generic pencil skirt pattern.

skirt panels are close to rectangular. The difference between the hip and waist measurements will tell you how many inches you'll need to remove from the top of the rectangle, either with darts, gathers, or just trimming the corners of the rectangle. You'll probably need more of this sort of tailoring in the back than in the front of the skirt.

A-LINE SKIRT

The pattern pieces for an A-line skirt look like pieces of pie with a curved bite taken from the point. When the pieces are assembled, the "bites" line up to form the circular opening for your waist. The difference between the top and bottom width of the

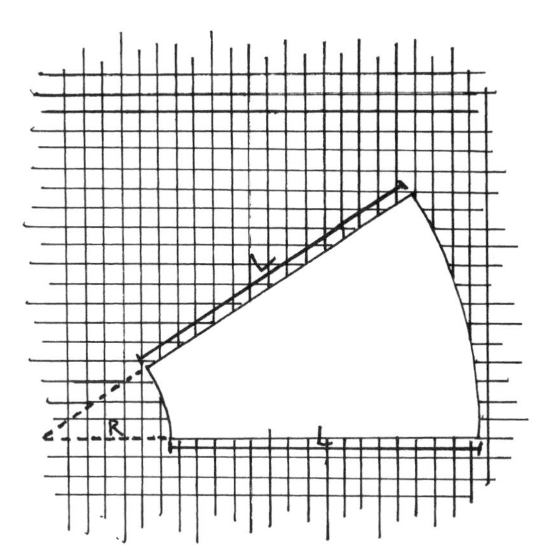

Drafting a pattern piece for an A-line skirt. R is the radius of a circle with the same circumference as your waist. L is the length of the skirt.

gores will determine how full the skirt is. If the gores are fairly straight, you may want to use some darts as well. An A-line skirt can have as few as two gores (front and back), or dozens.

The trickiest part will be putting the right curve on the bottom edge of each piece, so that when the pieces are all assembled they form one smooth, even edge, instead of scallops or points. One way to do this is to think of your skirt pieces laid out flat as a circle or semicircle. A very full skirt will form a full circle; a narrow A-line skirt might form a quarter circle (and will probably require darts). Decide what fraction of the circle your skirt forms (that is, a half, a third, or three-quarters of a circle), and call that fraction f. Call your waist measurement w. Then each of your pattern pieces will be approximately the illustrated shape, with r being the waist radius. (Note: If you are attaching the skirt to a dress, you need to measure the bottom of the dress's bodice, not your actual waist.)

$$r = w \div (f \times 2\pi)$$

This formula makes it easy to draft the pattern pieces. Lay out a large piece of paper (or several firmly taped together), draw the straight edges of your gore, then use a yardstick to mark several points that are r inches away from the corner point of the slice. Draw the arc that connects these points to form the waistline of this pattern piece. Then, much farther out, mark many points that are $r + l$ inches from the corner point of the slice, where l is the desired length of the skirt. Connect these points with an arc, and you will have the bottom edge of your pattern piece. Add seam allowances and room for zippers or buttons, and you will be ready to make the muslin mockup.

Of course, in spite of all these exact measurements, both cloth and the human body are soft and flexible. A-line skirts will necessarily have areas that are hanging on the bias of the fabric, which means they will stretch more than areas that are hanging with the grain. Furthermore, if you have a posterior of any sort, the back of the skirt will need to be slightly longer for the hem to be level. These variations will be most noticeable on shorter, narrower skirts. In any case, the hem is pretty much the last part of a dress or skirt to be finished, and the key here is to build in some excess and mark the final hem when the dress is actually on you.

10

Making Quilts

Historically, quilting has spanned the gap from luxury art to frugal recycling. Victorian ladies cut bits of satin and silk into impractical random shapes so they could employ their fanciest stitches in putting the pieces back together—these crazy quilts were quite a fad in the finest parlors everywhere. Later, frugal people modified the technique to use up odd scraps of cotton and wool. Of course, people were making quilts long before the Victorians, but these were generally composed of regular blocks or whole pieces of fabric (and, in fact, many crazy quilts are not even quilted).

Anyone who has witnessed a Mennonite quilt auction knows that quilts still inspire people with awe and a certain frenzied longing—a longing for Sunday afternoons, perhaps, and sunbeams falling across well-made beds. Quilting is one of the practical, frugal arts that our ancestors practiced with creativity and grace in the face of privation, and we're right to venerate it.

Technically, quilting refers to the process of stitching together multiple layers of fabric, but nowadays people often use the term to refer to patchwork in general. Patchwork is often quilted, but it doesn't have to be—and you can certainly quilt things that aren't patchwork.

Making a quilt involves two distinct steps. First, the pieces of the quilt top are cut and stitched together. Second, the top, batting, and backing are stacked on top of each other, and the layers are quilted in place.

You can study the art of quilt making quite deeply, and find out all the ways to make your work more intricate and precise, and you could fill multiple books with your knowledge. But I'm just going to give you a basic introduction here, with enough information to play around and figure things out for yourself. And no, you do not need a room-size quilting frame. A lap-size quilting hoop will do just fine.

Design

Unless you're making a crazy quilt (see page 209), you need to plan your quilt exhaustively. Take a look at the traditional patterns and adapt one or invent your own. Many pieced quilts are composed of thirty or so blocks, each in turn composed of nine squares (or triangles fitted together into squares). Breaking the quilt assembly into smaller units like this makes it significantly easier to get everything to line up right in the end.

The material you choose also impacts the quilt design. Fabric sold for quilting is a stiff, smooth cotton, but you can use fabric scraps from almost any type of material, provided it's not down-

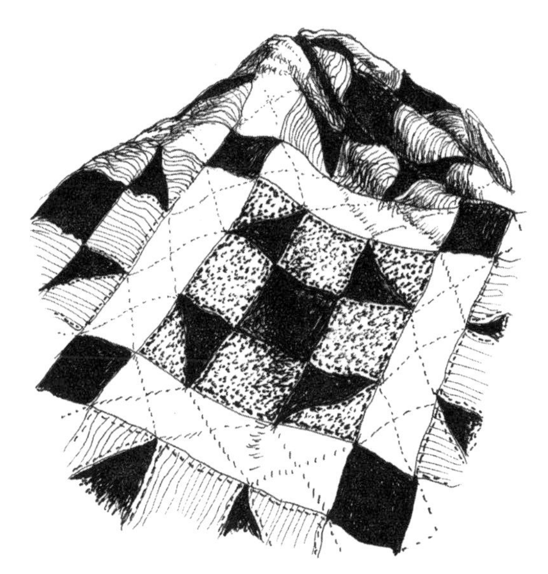

This traditional quilt block is called Philadelphia Pavement, with a Shoofly pattern in the center.

right stretchy or impenetrably thick. For any given quilt, your fabric should be fairly homogenous in thickness, weight, and weave—that is, don't try to mix denim scraps with sheer bits of silk. (If you do have a very thin material you'd like to use, you can layer it.) Some excellent sources of material: old wool blankets, children's outgrown clothing, and ripped-up jeans. Also check for fabric remnants at sewing stores. Above all, have fun finding complementary colors and patterns.

Making the Pattern Pieces

Once you've picked a design, do the math to figure out how big your finished pattern pieces need to be and what their shapes are. Your pieces can be triangles, squares, rectangles, or diamonds, or any other polygon, but they really should have straight sides, unless you want to do appliqué or have a lot of patience.

Speaking of patience, the smaller your pieces, the more work you'll have to do piecing them together. Most quilt squares are at least 2½ inches wide, with odd-shaped pieces proportional. Heavier material is better suited to large pieces; the smaller you cut the pieces, the more total fabric you have to use (seam allowances!), and the heavier the quilt becomes.

Carefully draft your pattern pieces on thin cardboard. Add ¼ to ½ inch of seam allowance on all sides (the larger amount for coarse weaves like denim and wool). If your pieces are squares or other neatly tessellating forms, you might find it easiest to draft a grid directly on your fabric. This is less practical if you're using fabric scraps, of course.

In any case, try to line up your pattern pieces with the grain of the fabric. That won't always be possible, of course, especially for nonsquare pieces. It's okay; fabric grain matters less with small quilt pieces than with garment pieces. Just take extra care when stitching together pieces on the bias, as they'll stretch out of proportion.

Piecing

Stitching the quilt pieces together is called piecing the quilt. It's an iterative process, in which you stitch the pieces into mini-quilts (blocks), then stitch the mini-quilts into one big quilt.

It's usually best to start with the smallest pieces. For example, if you're piecing a quilt like the one shown above, you would want to first stitch the triangular pieces together to form squares, then stitch three squares together in a row (and press; see page 177). Stitch the other six squares into two more rows, then stitch the three rows together (and press). One block finished! Repeat for the remaining blocks. Some patterns have long spacing pieces between each block; add these after you've stitched all the blocks.

Once all the blocks are stitched, you can start attaching them to each other. Use your pins to make sure all the pieces match up! It's helpful to stitch the blocks into rows, then stitch the rows together with one long seam. Some patterns, of course, have no obvious blocks at all. Treat them as if they did anyway.

Many quilts have large plain pieces around the edges. These are handy because they make the quilts significantly bigger without much extra work and they give the quilt a nice framing border. 'Sup to you. Add them at the end, if you do.

Quilting

To start quilting, you'll need to prepare your batting and backing. The batting is the layer of fluff inside a quilt that gives it a full, puffy texture. Strictly speaking, there doesn't *have* to be batting, but it does add significant warmth without a lot of extra weight. You can buy batting at fabric stores, but you can also use an old blanket (wool or fleece for the springiness). Customarily, batting is not very thick—¼ inch fluffed up, tops. If it's any thicker or denser, the quilting will take longer because you won't be able to make multiple stitches at once.

The backing is simply one large piece of material a couple of inches larger than the finished quilt on all sides. It can be pieced together from two or more sections of fabric (and will probably have to be if it's a fairly large quilt). But it should not be laboriously pieced together like the quilt top; use just a few straight seams. Pick a color that complements your quilt top, since it will show.

Working on a clean floor, lay out the backing (wrong side up), and spread the batting over it evenly. With big, lazy stitches, baste the batting together so it doesn't shift around and leave gaps. Now lay the pieced quilt top over the batting. Adjust everything very carefully so it's all lying flat and the layers are centered. The batting should come to the edge of the quilt top or extend a little farther, and the backing should be 2 inches larger on all sides.

Now, starting from the center, baste all three layers together with long, loose rows of stitches spaced every 12 inches or so. Smooth and readjust the quilt layers as you go to keep them aligned.

Have you decided on your quilting pattern? Your quilting stitches can follow the edges of your quilt pieces, crisscross them, or go off in fanciful swirls. The main thing that matters is that your quilting stitches will be evenly distributed across the pattern and close enough to hold the quilt securely together. Quilting directly on the seam lines is less structurally sound, but you can frame pieces with stitching ⅛ to ¼ inch from the edge.

Heavy materials in large pieces can be coarsely quilted with thick thread in rows stitched several inches apart. The look would certainly be more rustic. Finer patterns do well with quilting stitches closer to 2 inches apart. Look at other quilts or at pictures online to generate ideas. In the end, the closer your quilting pattern, the more time it will take, but the more secure the finished quilt will be.

To start quilting (finally!), position the smaller ring of your quilting hoop under the center of the quilt, push the top ring on from above, and tighten it well. You might want to lightly sketch your quilting pattern onto the fabric with a pencil, if you want your stitches to be quite straight. If you're using very thick thread and large stitches on heavy material, you might even do without the quilting hoop. Just work from the center out, and be very mindful of the layers shifting around on each other.

Load up your needle with thread—a matching color or not. Specially designated quilting thread is smooth and a little bit wiry, making it less vulnerable to fraying, snagging, and tangling. Ordinary thread is fine, too, and you could even use very thick thread or light string on something like denim.

Make a little knot in the end of the thread and poke the needle up through all three layers at your starting point. Hold the backing right by the knot and give a sharp little tug on your needle to pop the knot through the backing (but not through the other layers).

The quilting stitch is just a basic up-and-down running stitch following the predetermined lines. You should be able to poke the needle up and down several times, loading multiple stitches, before you pull the thread all the way through. This dramatically improves your efficiency. It's okay if quilting stitches aren't as even and precise as you'd like—such details will be lost in the general effect—but do try to keep them pretty small.

Complete all the stitching lines in the center of your frame before repositioning it to an adjacent area and moving on. Working too close to the edge of the frame will only be uselessly annoying. Keep quilting from the center of the quilt outward, as the layers will shift and distort slightly as you go.

Yes, this is a slow process. Work in a well-lit space, taking care not to hunch. Download an audiobook, or invite a friend over to chat or read aloud to you. I'm particularly fond of sewing while listening to old episodes of *Theme Time Radio Hour.*

Knotting

Knotting is the quick way to finish a quilt. It's not as secure as quilting, but it does the trick, and you can get it all done in a single sitting. Choose a yarn that makes a very solid knot. Load it up on an appropriately large needle. From the top, make a little stitch down and up through all the layers of the quilt. Pull the yarn through, leaving several inches on each side of the stitch. Snip it off and move on to the next one. The knots should be evenly and closely spaced—several inches apart.

If the pattern of your quilt permits it, you can space the knots on a perfect grid, 4 to 6 inches apart. Instead of snipping your thread between stitches, just pull it gently taut. Later you can snip the yarn halfway between each stitch and it'll be the proper length. Efficiency!

Once you've placed the yarn, go back and make all your knots. You want to make a strong, tight square knot or even a surgeon's knot. A surgeon's knot is just like a square knot, except the first time you put the thread through the loop, twist it around through the loop twice. Finish just like a square knot. Trim the loose ends of each knot to be 1 inch or so long.

Finishing

When you've finished quilting, go over the quilt and take out all the basting stitches that held it in place. Lay the quilt out on a clean floor and trim the batting to be flush with the edge of the quilt top. Things may have shifted a bit during the long quilting process. The backing should still be 2 inches larger than the quilt top and batting. Fold the backing down 1 inch (press it if it's being unmanageable) and then fold down again over the quilt top. Pin it in place, mitering the corners (like wrapping a present). It should form a nice, even 1-inch border around the quilt.

You can either whipstitch it to the quilt top or machine topstitch it, if it's not very thick.

There are other ways to finish a quilt—a common one is to create a separate edge strip about 4 inches wide. The strip gets machine stitched to just the quilt top, then folded over and handstitched to the quilt back with tiny stitches that don't penetrate to the quilt top. In this case, you would trim the backing flush with the quilt top and batting.

Crazy Quilts

Crazy quilting is a one-step process. You're piecing the quilt as you attach it to the backing.

Start by preparing your backing. It needs to be 2 inches larger than your eventual quilt on all sides, as described earlier. Now, get out your scraps. The scraps for a crazy quilt can be more diverse than the scraps for a regular quilt. You can use delicate fabrics like satins and lace along with sturdier materials (so long as you can still poke your needle through!). And of course, the shapes can be *almost* anything, though nothing should be more narrow than 1 inch or so, and you don't want any enormous pieces.

It will be easier to work on a large flat surface or with a quilting hoop. Lay two scraps down, overlapping by ½ inch or more along one edge. Fold under the overlapping edge of the top piece, ¼ to ½ inch. Pin it to the bottom piece and the backing, and stitch along the folded edge where the two pieces meet. Use colorful embroidery floss and break out your fanciest embroidery stitches here, if you like, or just do a simple whipstitch. The important thing is that you stitch through all layers of material to secure the overlapping edges of both scraps to the backing.

Grab another scrap, and place it on the quilt so it overlaps one of the existing pieces. Fold down the overlapping edge of the top piece, and repeat; as you proceed, you'll find odd spots that require creative overlapping. Don't leave any holes or raw edges! Mix up your stitches, too.

Once you fill in the backing all the way up to 2 inches from the edge, you can roll the edge and finish it as described earlier. But again, instead of a plain whipstitch or topstitch, try something fancy when stitching down the edge.

You can fill a crazy quilt with batting, if you like. You'll just need to baste it first to the backing so it doesn't scoot around on you. Remove the basting stitches when the quilt is done.

11
Rug Braiding

I've seen braided rugs suffer children and animals and the traffic in front of the kitchen sink for thirty years and still look cheerful and hale. I have seen braided rugs that survived fires when the carpet around them scorched. This immortality makes sense when you consider that a single rug might contain ten wool coats or half a dozen blankets. There really isn't a way to make fabric or fiber any denser than by braiding it and lacing it together.

One of my mother's first jobs out of college was actually teaching rug-braiding classes. When she taught me the summer before I went away to college, she stressed that the key to making durable heirloom rugs is *tension*. This is no ordinary braiding. The finished braid thrums with tension, and the braids are lashed together so tightly that the lacing buries itself deep within the wool, visible on neither side of the rug. The loops of the braids are pulled into each other so forcibly that if color doesn't distinguish individual rows, you might think it is a single woven mass. A well-made braided rug is stiff and heavy and doesn't begin to be floppy until it's at least fifty years old.

Material

Procuring Material

You can conceivably make braided rugs out of most kinds of material, but medium-thick wool works best for a number of reasons. Wool has a natural springiness that helps it hold together, stretches where it needs to, and feels nice underfoot. It's also a joy to work with, and that's something to consider, since you're going to be touching it *a lot.* You can use thin wool, too, but you'll have to roll it up extra when you're working with it in order for the strands to be thick enough. Those extra rolls and folds look less smooth and even and create spots that are more vulnerable to wear. Cotton can work, but it doesn't have the same forgiving bounce and stretch that wool does.

Wool blends are fine, and you can even use strips of straight-up synthetics in a mostly wool rug if they're a similar texture; just don't rely on them heavily or the overall effect of the rug will be synthetic. Above all, avoid mixing different fabric textures in the same rug.

You're going to need several big bundles of material. It would be quite expensive to buy your material new at $15 per yard or whatever nice thick wool is going for these days. Instead, keep an eye out for large wool garments and blankets at thrift stores and yard sales. Coats are a good source of wool, but they also tend to be heavily reinforced and tailored, making them a pain to tear apart and cut up. Blankets are by far the easiest source of wool, and sometimes you can get huge wool surplus blankets for a decent price. Just be careful that they're not too thick; you want a material that can fold fairly easily. Avoid small bits of wool with distinctive colors or patterns. You won't easily be able to match it, and a small skirt, say, might not even have enough material to make a complete ring in your rug. Of course, a righteous blaze of unmatched colors may be your intention.

A lot of useful wool gets donated to thrift stores but never makes it onto the rack. Maybe it has a few holes or worn spots, but the bulk of the material is fine. This is gold, and local thrift stores might even be persuaded to save it for you and give it away or sell it by the pound. Nationally run operations, like Goodwill, have big centralized distribution centers where all their donations go. Sometimes these as-is outlets are open to the public, where you can go and paw through enormous unsorted bins of stuff in search of the cheapest wool. Be careful, though! There are people who make a living competitively scrounging through those bins for antiques, electronics, and fancy clothing to sell on eBay. Don't try to compete with them, and take courage that they are most definitely not looking for old wool blankets.

Since you'll be working in a long spiral from the center of the rug out, each successive ring in the rug will be longer and require more material to finish. In other words, you'll need lots and lots of any color you want on the outside of the rug, but you can get away with just having a piece or two of a certain color you want toward the middle of the rug.

Furthermore, there are gorgeous patterns you can only make

on relatively straight stretches of the rug—these patterns are restricted to the broad circles on the outside edges of round rugs or the straight sides of oval rugs. These patterns also require that two of your strands be the same color. In other words, you'd need massive quantities of that color.

You can see that it would be helpful if some of the main colors in your rug are common and easy to find—charcoal, black, red, or beige, for example. That said, the 1980s left behind a glut of brilliant colored garments, which are now finding their way into thrift stores.

In general, solid colors give the rug a bold clarity, whereas plaids and heathers give it more softness.

Preparing the Material

Making your braiding strips is definitely the most boring and least rewarding part of braiding rugs. The more large, flat pieces of fabric you start with, the quicker this stage of the project will go. But sometimes you really want a particular shade of green, and all you can find in that color is an old wool coat with tons of tailoring and buttons and a lining to rip out.

By no means do you have to prepare all your strips before you start working on the rug. It can be a back-and-forth process of tearing up coats to incorporate in your growing rug as you go, and in fact, putting the rug together will give you a clearer notion of what colors you need and how much of them.

Wash your material first (in *cold* water; no felting, please!) and line dry it. Washing particularly helps with the dust that's sure to fly when you start ripping up the seams of coats that have hung in an attic for ten years. You might even want to rip out linings and pull open sleeves before washing so the deep dust really gets flushed out. For me, at least, this part of the process is one long sneeze-fest.

To make your strips, lay out your fabric and note the line of the grain. The easiest and most satisfying way to make strips is to cut a little notch in one edge of the fabric and then just rip it along the grain. However, depending on its shape, ripping along the grain line might not be the most efficient use of the fabric, and it's okay to cut your strips with scissors so long as they're close to lining up with the grain (avoid cutting strips on the bias).

You want all your strips to be a consistent thickness when rolled up tight, so the width of your strips depends on the thickness of the fabric. Around 2 inches is the minimum width you want to work with, for a decently thick wool. Thinner wools should be cut in strips 3 inches or wider.

Steer around any holes. If they're small and right near the edge of a strip, they probably don't matter, but even tiny holes in the middle of the strip can make the rug wear out much more quickly.

Once you've amassed a pile of strips of one color, it's time to attach them to each other. A straight seam would create an awkward bulge in the strip. Instead, stitch a diagonal seam. Overlap the ends of two strips arranged perpendicularly, as shown in the illustration below. By hand or by machine, stitch the diagonal from one corner to the other, securing the stitch at each end. Trim off the corner ¼ inch from the seam. When you unfold the joined pieces, you'll have one long strip with a diagonal seam that distributes its bulk over several inches.

Remember to keep all your seams on one side of the strip! It's

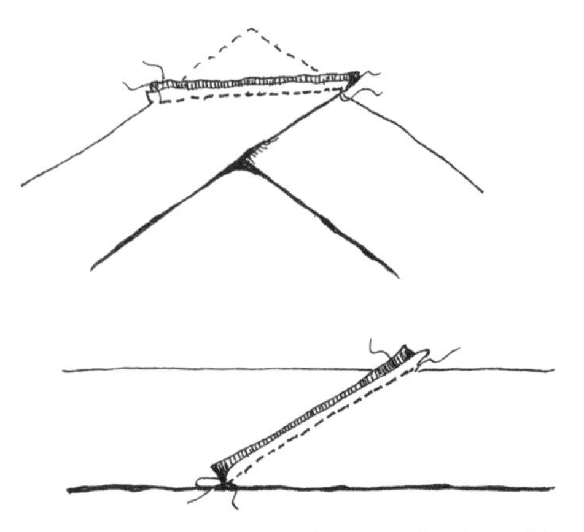

Unfolded, the strips will be straight, joined by a diagonal seam.

inevitable that at some point your strip will twist itself without your noticing, and you'll attach some pieces backward. Just keep an eye out and undo the flipped seam as soon as you notice it.

Once your strip is quite long, start coiling it up. Face the seam side inward, and keep the strip flat as you coil it around itself tightly. Once your coil reaches about 8 inches in diameter, it's time to start a new coil, or it will be too awkward to handle when braiding.

Equipment for Braiding and Lacing

You'll need a midsize C-clamp to clamp the braid to a table and a sturdy clip to hold the end of your braid whenever you stop braiding. For lacing, you'll need a bodkin, which is a flat, blunt-ended needle with a curved nose for lacing the braids together (readily available on the Internet or in well-stocked craft stores). Your lace itself is strong waxed linen or hemp twine, 1 to 2 millimeters thick. The wax gives it better grip on the wool.

You'll also want to make yourself a pair of finger guards for the middle two fingers of your dominant hand. These should be ½-inch-wide bands of leather or heavy fabric that fit snugly around your middle finger and ring finger. You'll be pulling so hard on the lacing that without these guards your fingers will get cut.

Braiding Technique

I'm going to first describe the braiding technique that you'll use for the majority of the rug. The very center of the rug, where you start, uses a specialized braid that's easier to master if you've first figured out the regular braid.

Set yourself up at a comfortable table you can clamp your braid to. Set the coils of strips in your lap, and pull the ends out a few feet long. Next, fold the edges of one strip in to the middle, seam side inward. Fold it again to make a snug little roll. Slide a large safety pin through it and repeat with the two other strips, sliding them on to the same pin with their open sides facing the same direction. Clamp the ends of the strips and the safety pin onto the table.

You know how to braid, right? Put the left strand over the middle strand. Then put the right strand over the new middle strand, and so on. Braiding rugs works the same way, except there are several other things to do simultaneously.

Braid tightly, folding the strands as you go and keeping the open edge to the left.

First, the braid needs to be very tight. You should be pulling away from the clamp, hard, as you work. When you're working under that much tension, however, any uneven tugging or slackening quickly makes the braid lopsided. You need to keep a firm, steady grip on all three strands as you work. As the rug grows, you won't need to clamp it anymore. You can sit on the floor, throw one leg over the rug, and work that way.

Second, keep each strip rolled as you braid—edges to the middle, then folded in half. As you unspool your coils of wool strips, keep feeding them into this position.

Third, you need to keep the open edge of each strand facing to the left. It's very important that you don't twist or fold the strands as you work—the open edge stays to the left as you weave the strand back and forth in the braid. You also want to try your best to keep the surface of each strand smooth and taut. If the strand starts to fold, pull it flat and tuck the open edge in tighter.

Finally, keep your clip at the ready. You'll need to untangle your coils quite frequently as you go, so be sure to clip the end of your braid securely to keep all that tension in place. You'll also have to scoot your chair back as the braid grows longer, and eventually you'll need to reclamp the braid.

As you can see, this is a lot to do, and there's nothing wrong with braiding a few feet for practice and then undoing it all. Several times.

Untangling the coils of wool is cumbersome, and I keep trying to invent some sort of lightweight ratcheted spool that would let the coils hang free from the braid without unraveling. But then they would get in the way of the braiding—and if they were long enough to stay out of the way, they'd be long enough to tangle anyway. The trick is to tell stories so entertaining that a helpful friend or child will have the patience to sit around untangling them for you as you go.

Starting a Rug

Once you're comfortable with the braiding technique, you can embark on a project. You'll first want to decide on the eventual shape of your rug. I'm going to describe a circular project right now, but you'll find descriptions of oval and rectangular and bizarre shapes later on.

A small circular chair pad is one of the canonical first projects for rug braiding, simply because it involves all the techniques you'll need to learn but avoids the miles and miles of braiding in between the start and finish of a big project. That said, a large project is really no more difficult than a small one. Just longer.

To start the braid, you'll need to form a butt end on each prepared strip. First fold the strip in half inside out. Make an L-shaped stitch as shown below, keeping about ¼ inch away from the raw end of the strip. Clip off the corner and turn the strip right-side out. You'll have a little finger on the end with no raw edges exposed.

Do this for all three of your strips and slide them on a large safety pin. Stitch the butt ends tightly together, keeping your stitches near the seam lines where they will be hidden when the braids are laced together.

There isn't enough braid yet to put it in the clamp, so you'll have to manage as best you can until the braid is a few inches long.

The tightly coiled center of a rug is braided differently from the wider loops farther out. In fact, the innermost coils are so tight that a good stiff straight braid can't possibly bend so much. The solution is a crooked braid, called an apple peel braid.

Braid once normally—left over center, right over center. Then braid an apple peel: left over center, right over center, right over center. This puts a kink in the braid. Continue alternating normal and apple peel braids until you have a braid several inches long that coils back on itself nicely. Now you can braid normally, throwing in an apple peel here and there to help the braid curl—but remember that it's the nature of wool to bend and flex, so incorporate the apple peels sparingly. Don't go more than 6 inches before you start lacing.

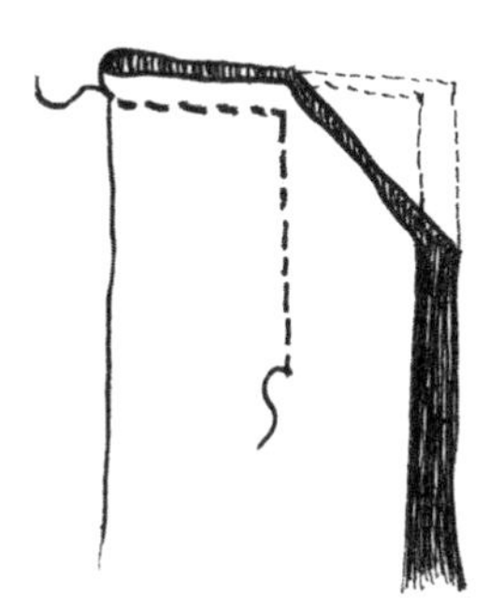

The L-shaped seam forms a pocket, which becomes the butt end of the braiding strip when turned inside out.

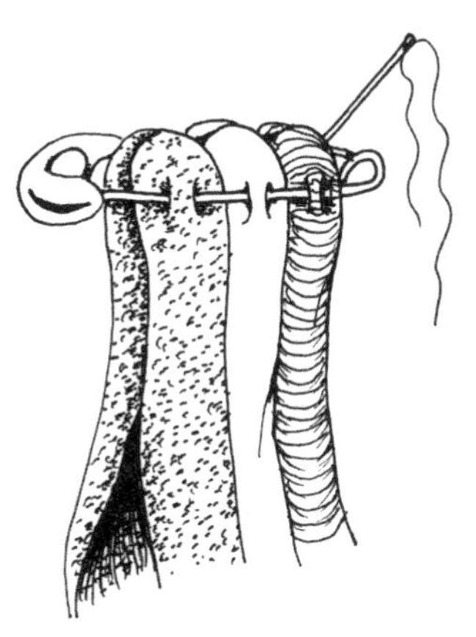

Slide the three butt ends onto a safety pin, seams facing left.

The white strip and the dotted strip get an extra twist, forming an apple peel braid.

Lacing

Starting the Lace

Load several feet of waxed linen on your bodkin and turn your braid upside down. The braid should now be curling counterclockwise from the center. Slip the bodkin up through the first or second braid loop on the butt end on the inside of the corner. (See the lacing illustration, facing, to see what I mean by *up through*; it's almost more sideways than up.) Do not pierce the material itself; hook the bodkin *around* the braid strand. Pull the twine most of the way through and slip the bodkin up through the braid loop across from it in the curl—this is probably just two or three loops farther down the braid.

Holding on to the loose end of your twine, pull it very, very taut and tie it in a tight knot. Poke the knot with the end of your bodkin until it pops inside a braid loop (make sure it's not visible from the other side, either). Continue lacing as described in the next section.

General Lacing

Always turn the rug upside down to lace it. The backward braid loops on the underside of the rug make it easier to lace tightly. Put on your finger guards. Insert the bodkin at the side of the braid and follow the braid loop so the bodkin pops out in the center of the braid. Hook your middle two finger around the twine and pull tightly, so tightly that the braid loops fuse into each other and the twine disappears completely. Then insert

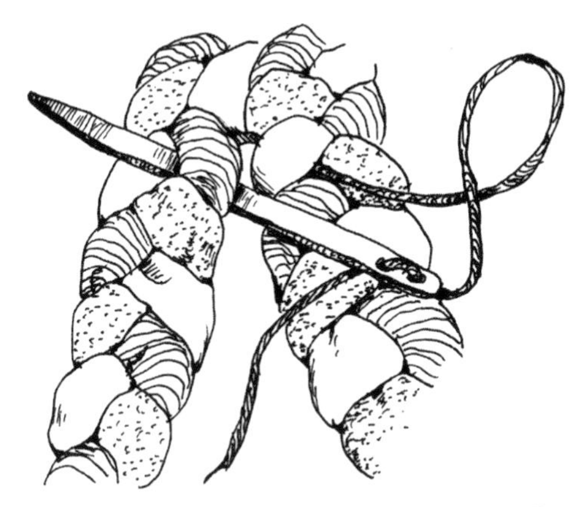

Turn the rug upside down and lace back and forth around each braid loop on both braids. The bodkin enters on the underside and pops out in the middle of the braid.

the bodkin into the braid loop directly across from the one you just looped—you might even be going backward slightly. Pull it tight, and repeat.

If you're lacing correctly, you will be lacing through every single braid loop on both braids, but because the outer ring is larger than the previous one, you'll need to skip one outer braid loop every so often. Be consistent about how often you skip a loop; at first you might be skipping every fourth or fifth loop, but later you will be skipping every twenty or more. If you skip too frequently, the edge of the rug will buckle and scallop. If you don't skip enough, it will turn into a bowl. Don't worry; even a wavy, wobbly rug will lie flat after a month or two.

It is incredibly important that the lacing be tight, tight, tight. The laced braid loops will actually intertwine with each other, creating a new braid-like effect between the two braids. If the lacing is not tight enough, the rug will be significantly weaker, as the floppiness will put strain on individual strands of lacing, rather than distributing the strain evenly across all the twine.

When you run out of twine, firmly knot a new piece onto it. When you come to the knot while lacing, give a sharp tug to pop it under a braid loop and hide it from view. Make sure it's not visible on the other side, either—poke it around with your bodkin to get it just right, and check that when you tug the lace later it doesn't pop it into view.

Changing Colors

To switch to a new roll of wool or a new color, trim the end of the braid strand at 45-degree angle, and trim the end of the new strip at the corresponding angle. Right side to right side, stitch the ends together to form a diagonal seam much like when you were forming the original strips, but be sure to keep the strips centered if they're of significantly different widths. Continue braiding, and when you come to the new seam, try to shift the braid around so the seam is on a hidden part of the strand.

Finishing a Rug

Since a braided rug is a continuous spiral, laced back to itself, you might wonder how you can possibly end it. There are several options. The first is the rattail: You trim the last 8 inches or so of each strip to form a gradual taper down to a point. Braid as far as you can, maintaining the folds and all, until you can't braid any longer without the raw strip edges popping out. Clip the end of the braid and lace up to the end. Then use pliers or a crochet hook to grab one of the strands and weave it into a braid loop of matching color on the previous ring. Give the other strands a twist, and tuck them into their corresponding colors. Trim any ends that hang out, and with matching thread, make a few stitches to be sure each strand is securely tucked.

The second finishing method is to form a rattail, but follow it with a butted row, which gives a nice finished border to the rug and looks like a circular continuous braid. Magical! And rather tricky.

Start braiding the final ring just the way you started the rug, but don't stitch the three strands together. Keep them securely fastened with a clip or safety pin. When you go to lace the ring to the rug, leave the first 6 inches or so unlaced. Continue around as usual until you reach the starting point, leaving the last few inches unlaced as well.

Now you need to make the start and the end into a continuous braid. Braid the end until the strands are in the same arrangement as they are at the start. Mark the point where each ending strand would meet its corresponding beginning strand. Undo the braid a little way and trim the wool strips ½ inch beyond this point. Fold under the ½-inch end and fold in the sides of the strip; stitch in place. Rebraid the end and clamp.

You should have two butt-end braids that match up. Now, this whole butted-braid process involves lots of patience and the ability to will fabric into its proper place. Your job is to stitch each strip to its matching strand on the other side, maintaining the braided pattern while you do. There should be no slack excess material, no bumps and puffs. But there probably will be the first

Line up the matching pairs of butt ends and wrangle them into place.

time you try it, or maybe you'll realize it's not a braid by the time you're done. It's one of those precarious things where nothing holds together in its proper place until everything is done. Don't be afraid to redo it until it looks right.

Once the butted braid is stitched together, you can lace the rest of it to the rug. Secure and disguise your lacing twine by knotting it back on itself, lacing it through several more loops, and trimming it flush.

Shapes

An oval braided rug is more accurately a rectangle with two half circles on each end. You start the rug by braiding a long straight strip the length of the finished rectangle. When it's time to turn the corner back, use a few apple peel braids. You'll really only need the apple peel on the first two corners.

You can make a rectangular rug by braiding separate strips side by side or by forming four sharp apple peel corners every time you go around. Beyond that, you can come up with all sorts of shapes once you're comfortable with the mechanics.

Patterns

When you're lacing long straight sections of a rug, you don't have to skip any loops. This lets you create patterns formed by lacing together matching colors. You can even form these patterns on circular rugs provided you're working 20 inches or so out from the center, where consecutive rows have a fairly small difference in length. Here, again, we are relying on the wonderful elasticity of wool to even things out for us when we force the strands to go where we want.

With three different colors, you can create an interesting pattern by lacing matching colors together. With just two colors—two strands of black and one of red, for example—you can either create a web-like pattern by never letting red touch red, or a black diamond pattern by matching the reds together.

These patterns can be repeated indefinitely on straight stretches, and for several rows on round areas. The shallower the curve (the farther out you are on a circular rug) the more patterned rows you can put together. At some point, however, you'll have to go back to skipping loops when you lace, or the rug will become bowl shaped. Start a new pattern or do something random for a while. When you're starting a large patterned section on a curved part of the rug, it helps to skip a few extra loops on the first row. That way you've built in some excess.

Caring for the Finished Rug

Like I said, braided rugs are eminently sturdy. Clean them with a wet sponge or a bristly brush. If the rug has any warp to it, keep it in a clean but well-trafficked spot. It will become perfectly flat within a short amount of time.

12
Gardening

The art of growing food is beautiful and righteous, but apart from the basics like watering and fertilizing, so much of the best advice depends on regional factors, like climate and soil. And so we offer you a handful of project plants—plants that are hardy and construction ready, like gourds and bamboo, and small plants with a big payoff, like herbs and (goodness!) tobacco.

Bamboo

People will tell you "Don't plant bamboo, it will take over everything." True, but it is the most versatile of plants and in my opinion the most beautiful, too. What else grows to height in a week or two; can be eaten; and can made into instruments, chopsticks, and building timbers. Not to mention formed into great cutting boards or laminated flooring. I don't know how the latter are made, but here are some great things to do with bamboo.

When it first comes up, snap off the shoots, remove the outer tough fronds, simmer them briefly in water, and serve like asparagus. They can also be tossed on the grill whole and seasoned with a little vinaigrette. If you have really fat ones, slice them up, soak to remove the bitterness, and add to a stir-fry. The taste is so fresh and green, you will never want to eat a tinny bamboo shoot from a can again. They are also delicious marinated in oil and vinegar and can even be pickled in brine. The trick is, you have to catch them in the first few days they sprout up.

If they get bigger, then let them grow to full size and make some flutes. Cut a few poles and let them thoroughly dry or else they may split when you try to work with them. I leave mine in a corner of the house for a full year. With a small handsaw, cut a section with a node at each end. The width doesn't matter; smaller ones will give you a high pitch and wide ones a low, sonorous woody tone. Next heat up an iron rod on the barbecue—a shish kebab skewer or a large iron spit is best—and poke through the interior segments with the hot rod on one end only. It will take a few pokes to burn through each node. Leave the final one intact and closed. At this point you can make several of these of different lengths, strap them together, don your goatskin and pretend you're Pan ("Pan, Pan, Greek god Pan; one half goat, the other half man") or just hang them on strings and let them bump in the breeze. A great wind chime.

You can also burn holes into the sides to make a real flute. There should be one wide opening near the closed top to serve as the mouthpiece. Map these others out by placing your fingers in a comfortable position. Mark with a pencil and then burn through holes. You can also use a drill if you like, but it's a little more tricky to do without splitting the bamboo. When done, blow across the top hole and lift one finger at a time on the lower holes. You now know how to play the flute. The hard part is getting a full Western scale. Because the diameter of each piece is so variable, there's really no way to hit it right, except for chance. But you will have beautiful whole tone scales if you space them evenly. I have had the best luck with *Phyllostachys bambusoides*, a giant variety that has a diameter of 4 to 5 inches. I cut a section to 1½ to 2 feet and put seven holes spaced exactly where my fingers are comfortable. Perfect major scale.

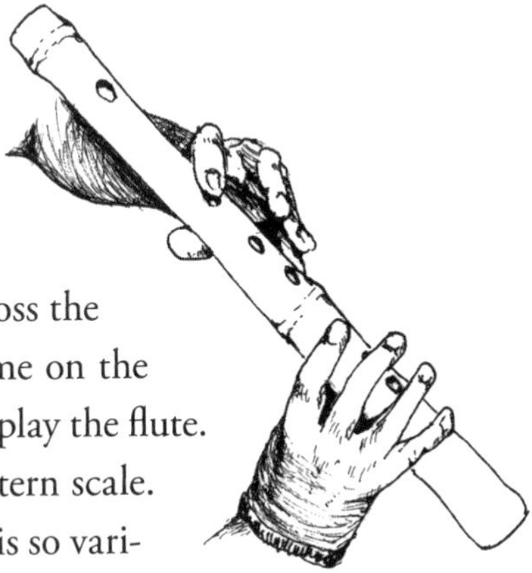

From your bamboo you can also cut fresh green chopsticks, which are really delightful to eat with. Or save the poles and use them for building projects. Strapped together with ropes, they make a great teepee frame, a larger tent, or if you're ambitious a full-scale yurt in which you can sip your yak butter tea. Or even better, fling yourself from pole to pole and play Crouching Tiger, Hidden Dragon.

—K

Tobacco

I swear that this tobacco is perfect Trinidad-o. By the very very Mass, never never was better gear than is here, by the rood, for the blood, it is very very good, 'tis very good.

—Thomas Weelkes

I know that in this age of health consciousness, those among you will chide me for including information on this vile weed. Nor is this attitude new; when tobacco became all the rage in the late sixteenth and early seventeenth centuries in England, King James himself composed a diatribe against the custom, which he found pernicious and barbaric. But try to imagine the excitement tobacco first stirred, when physicians lauded it for coughs and lung ailments, when stimulants of any kind were unknown (including coffee and tea). Or think of the sacred role of tobacco in Native American cultures. You may be inspired to grow some.

You can find seeds online, and the plants themselves produce delicate white trumpet-shaped flowers, closely related to decorative *Nicotiana* as well as other Solanacea-like tomatoes and peppers. But in this case, you want the leaves to grow big, so diligently pinch off the buds before they flower. There are many ways to cure the leaves; essentially you want to hang them in a warm humid place with good airflow. A barn in the South is ideal, but you can hang them in the kitchen, too, for just a few weeks. You may also want to age them so they mellow, just be sure they don't dry out too much. You don't want them too moist, either, or they'll rot. Once they're lightly brown and still supple, you can twist up the whole leaf into a cord, fold in half and then twist that again into a coil. This is the shape you always see in old paintings, and they still do it this way in Kentucky. If you're at sea, or any place windy, we recommend just biting off a bit and chewing it. Or you can remove the larger ribs and finely shred the leaves for pipe tobacco or to be rolled. Or finely chop it and make a Scandinavian-style moist snus chewing tobacco (like Copenhagen). Or if you're very adventurous, grind the dry leaves into a fine powder, put a little dab on the fleshy part of your hand between thumb and forefinger and snort it up. This is called sneeshing in Scotland—or snuff elsewhere.

—K

Gourds

Although gourds are edible, they don't taste like much of anything. Don't confuse these with New World squashes, which are all delicious. Gourds are in the genus *Lagenaria*, the seeds of which, unlike squashes, are not smooth but look like little Martian pods, and are equally uninteresting to eat. So I suggest using gourds as our ancestors did—as storage vessels. Even if you don't grow them, they are well worth buying if you see them around Halloween; they are big, green, and bottle shaped. The last one I bought is the size and shape of a goose. You can let them dry on their own, but I suggest cutting off an end or across the narrow middle. Scoop out the insides and then just wait. The gourd will dry and become hard all on its own. Then the fun part: decoration. You can use a wood-burning pen or simply take an old steak knife bent into an interesting shape, heat the tip on the stove and burn a funky tribal pattern into the gourd. Some people paint gourds and lacquer them, but we want to use ours. So

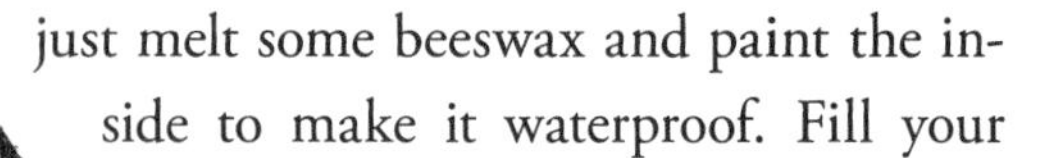

just melt some beeswax and paint the inside to make it waterproof. Fill your gourd at the stream and carry it back to the village on your head humming a plaintive melody.

—K

Herb Gardening

When I used to work in grocery stores, I would sometimes give people scrap-box snips of cilantro or parsley if they only needed a sprig and didn't want to buy the whole bunch and have it go to waste. What I *should* have done, of course, is send them home with the entire bunch and a good recipe for tabbouleh or pesto. If it was a single twig of rosemary the customer wanted, however, I had somewhat less generosity. Our fair city is abundantly hedged with perfectly delicious rosemary bushes, and anyway, rosemary keeps much longer than cilantro.

Many grocery store workers enforce the rules more literally than I did. That leads to a yucky, wasteful problem: whole bunches of herbs moldering away weeks after they were purchased, abandoned after providing a sprig or two for a particular recipe. (Note: There is lots of advice about keeping fresh herbs, but the simplest to me is to hang them up in small bunches in a dry, well-ventilated space. Freshly dried herbs are not as good as fresh herbs, of course, but they're far better than store-bought dried herbs.)

The solution is to grow your own convenient pot of herbs, the obvious first choice for gardening in limited spaces. Not only can you plant a convenient variety of herbs in a large pot or two on an apartment fire escape or sunny window, but you can avoid the hassle and waste of buying entire bunches of eminently perishable herbs like cilantro.

There are two general categories of herbs: annuals and perennials. The annuals will need to be torn up and replanted every few months when they go to seed. The shrubby perennials may want to be pruned from time to time but are otherwise fairly low maintenance.

Preparing the Pot

The tricky part of container gardening is regulating the water. Pots can dry out more quickly than the earth, but they also trap excess moisture and rot the plants if they're overwatered. Larger pots attenuate this effect.

Make sure your pot has one or more good drainage holes and a deep dish or tray to set it in. Arrange a layer or two of paper over the bottom and partially up the sides of the pot. Newspaper or scrap paper will work fine; avoid glossy or heavily dyed paper. This will keep soil from rinsing out through the drainage holes until the roots are established enough to keep a good grip on the soil.

Put a layer of stones or large gravel over the paper to aid in drainage. This keeps the bottom of the pot from becoming a soggy root-rotting swamp.

Fill in the rest of the pot with potting soil and maybe some extra fertilizer or compost if the potting soil isn't supplemented with it. Water it gently to compress it and add more potting soil to bring the dirt level up to the top of the pot.

Procuring Plants

It's cheapest and easiest to grow most herbs from seeds. Some herbs like rosemary, however, have a very low germination rate and can be quite tricky to sprout. Because rosemary is a perennial, you only need to buy it once, making it worthwhile to buy a start. For many shrubby perennials, you can also dig up a clump of a friend's plant, if you're so lucky.

You should most definitely get seed packets of plants like parsley and cilantro. Then you can conveniently replant them throughout the year. Other herbs easily grown from seed include mint, basil, thyme, sage, dill, poppies, and oregano; thyme and sage are perennials, though, and dill and poppies reseed themselves so prolifically that they're practically perennials.

Poppies don't fit in the usual fresh herb category, but they're so beautiful and easy to grow, and the freshness of poppy seeds is so important that I include them here. In fact, you may have only ever tasted bitter, rancid poppy seeds, since they deteriorate so quickly on grocery store shelves and in spice cabinets. However, you'd have to grow at least half a dozen big plants to get a decent quantity of seeds, and the seeds used for baking come only from the opium poppy, *Papaver somniferum*. The legality is a funny issue, since the plants are widely grown, the seeds are readily available, the world is well populated with poppy-seed baked goods, and yet U.S. law says they're not allowed.

Planting, Tending, and Harvesting

Follow seed packet directions for planting your herbs. Some temperature-sensitive seeds like basil should only be started indoors. In any case, germinating seeds need regular, light watering and mild conditions.

To transplant starts, dig them up or pop them out of their containers and massage open their roots. Plant them in a hole deep enough to keep them at the same soil level as they were in their pots. Plants like sage and rosemary will eventually need pots of their own, but they can share pots for a time.

All herbs have different requirements. Mint likes to be quite wet, for example, whereas sage and rosemary can handle long stretches without water if their pots are large enough and the weather is not too hot. Your climate will dictate how you care for your plants, when and where you can plant them, whether you must bring them in for the winter or keep them shaded in the summer, and how often you must water them.

Avoid harvesting herbs before they're reasonably well established. Some hardy herbs respond well to a vigorous harvest—for example, plants in the mint family (like sage) will rapidly grow new buds when picked. Still, try not to take more than a quarter of a plant at any picking, and give it a chance to regenerate before taking more.

And whatever you do, don't completely block up your fire escape. Heaven forfend, but it may come in handy some day.

—R

13

Building Projects

Here we offer some ideas for inveterate putterers, those of us who are happiest getting very messy by making stuff. You might argue that building and tinkering are hardwired into our genes, at least since the time of our hominid ancestor *Homo habilis*, the original handyman. These are not your typical hammer-and-nail or fix-a-washer-in-the-faucet kind of jobs though; they are ambitious and as antiquated as we could make them in the modern world. They are meant to inspire rather than intimidate. Most important, they are the kind of work in which you can get lost; hours pass happily, and in the end you have something both beautiful and functional, both craft and art.

Pottery

When I was in graduate school in New York City, I got it in my head that I wanted to make pottery. So I took throwing lessons with a woman named Maxine (I never knew her last name, or maybe she didn't have one, like Cher). A few years later I apprenticed, learning how to mix glazes, fire the kilns, and recycle clay. It was hard work, but proves the adage that the best way to learn is by doing. When I moved to California the first thing I did was set up a garage studio, now in the basement of my current home. Let me be clear though, I have never sold a single piece and I consider myself an amateur. Though I am convinced that this is such an easy and rewarding thing to do, and that once you've learned the basics, it is absolutely simple. And there is nothing more pleasant than eating off your own plates every day, drinking out of your favorite teacup, or even better, going over to friends' houses and spotting pots you made years before.

I am including this section not because I expect everyone to rush out and spend a few thousand dollars on a wheel and kiln (although I was given some secondhand equipment for free and have given away some myself since), but because pottery is so integral a part of what I do in the kitchen that I hope I may inspire some of you to follow suit. I also want you to understand that though the forms I make are historically derived, there is nothing particularly antiquated about the techniques I use. Zoning codes won't allow me to use gas, let alone a wood-burning kiln. The small scale of my studio also makes mixing my own glazes unfeasible, so I buy them. So if you professionals will turn a blind eye while I fire up my cone 6 electric kiln, I'll explain why pottery is so important to cooking and serving food—oh and decorating, too. And don't forget presents!

First, there are mixing bowls, pitchers and jugs, jars and crocks—a whole slew of utilitarian things you can make rather than buy. When they break, you make more. Second, there is something about the industrial mass-manufactured aesthetic that bugs me. Every stark white plate exactly the same regardless of the food served on it. Even at the best restaurants, the plates are a bore. Think of how traditional Japanese cuisine approaches the plates and bowls, every one slightly different, designed to hold a specific quantity and texture of a specific recipe. In fact, I think the pot and the recipe should be designed together. For example, dumplings go best in a shallow soup plate in which you can press down to cut the ingredients. Tapas sit best in small round plates, with sloping sides if they are sauced. Some recipes call for broad bases, some for narrow elegant ones, all of which makes a difference, just like when tasting wine. Speaking of

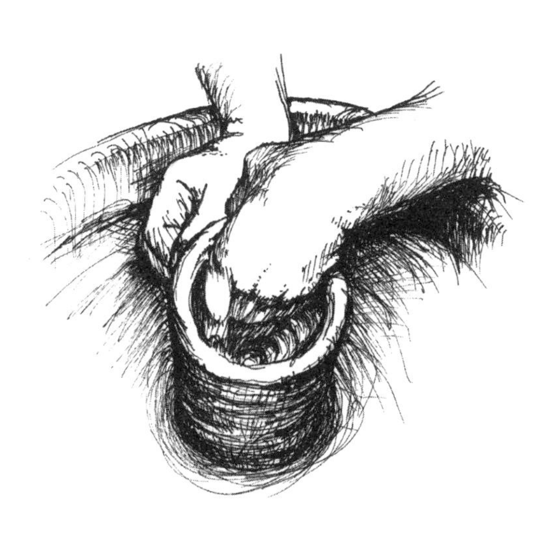

which, drinking wine from a capacious goblet you can actually hold onto with your whole hand is an indescribable pleasure.

Assuming you have taken lessons, in a studio, at college, or at your community center, you know how to throw; you are centered, so to speak. Though I do contend teaching someone to throw a simple pot takes only a few minutes. You wedge the clay, throw it hard onto the center of the dry wheel. Wet it, then kick or accelerate with both hands on the clay until you have a cylinder that no longer wobbles. Plunge in both thumbs, and with left hand inside at four o'clock and right hand outside, gently lift the wall until you have a soup can. That's the basic technique for almost everything. Widen the top for a bowl, bulge the base from the inside for a mug, then narrow the neck for a bottle. Trim when leather hard. I know this can't be taught with words, it has to be experienced. I just want to convey to you that it is not difficult at all, and there is no reason not to jump in. At the very least, toss your mass-produced soulless plates and bowls and support your local potter. Using beautiful vessels really does make food taste better.

—K

A Proper Dehydrator

I was sent off one day to buy a dehydrator. Fortunately no such thing can be bought in the city where I live. So I resolved to build one and spend as little money as possible on it. I understand this is not an option if you live somewhere wet and rainy, but given the Mediterranean climate of the Central Valley, it's almost a sin not use the sun's power. Begin by purchasing some cheap furring strips. They're usually spruce or pine, 8 feet long, 2 inches by 1 inch. This is not fine cabinetry, so don't worry if they're not perfect. They should cost about $1 each. You'll need six. You can make the rack the full 8 feet long, but 6 feet can be more easily lifted. Saw off 2 feet from each piece and then cut these in half into 12-inch crossbars. Lay two of the long pieces on the ground on the narrower edge and measure out where the crossbars will go. You will be making a kind of ladder for the lower half of the contraption, which will hold the fruit in place. With a tiny drill bit, drill guiding holes where you will screw in the crossbars (otherwise the wood will split) from the outer edge inward, to hold the rungs in place. Use two screws on each or the rungs will swivel. Then using stainless-steel (or brass) wood screws, screw in the rungs of the ladder from top to bottom.

Then make the top of the frame without rungs or with just a crossbeam in the center. Then cut a length of screening to fit the top and bottom; either staple the screen in place or use brass tacks, which look nice. Then attach three small hinges to connect the upper and lower frames. Be sure to staple the screen to every rung, or your fruit will slide down. You can also use duct tape to cover the sharp edges. Fill the lower frame with tomatoes, peaches, apple slices, anything you wish. Close the top frame and put the whole thing on the roof and leave there for about 1 week in the sun. You will impress your neighbors; it looks like a solar panel. I guess it is. After a week you can eat the dried fruits as is, dunk them in a bottle of vodka, or cook with them. Put the tomatoes in olive oil; a perfect way to preserve summer's bounty. If you happen to leave your tomatoes out too long and they become completely dry and brittle, don't worry. Crush them in a mortar or whizz in a spice grinder. You'll have a fine tomato powder, which is wonderful to use in soups or on salads, or sprinkled on a steak for marvelous effect. The exact same thing can be done with dried mushrooms.

—K

Fornax: Oven Goddess

I have spent many furtive nights, asleep and awake, dreaming about building a bread oven. I imagined running out late at night and just piling up mud, like the guy in *Close Encounters of the Third Kind*. Patiently, I consulted books, asked experts, some of whom are good friends. Do I go for the simple Paleolithic cob oven, the adobe horno of the Southwest, or a proper brick bread oven with industrially made materials? Directions for a simple earth oven can be found anywhere. There are many excellent books, so there was no reason to replicate them here. The industrial brick oven would, frankly, cost a fortune and would require professional plans. Initially my resolve was to spend no money: dig local clay, work it by foot with sand and straw like an Egyptian slave, mold it by hand, and fire in place. Clay is plentiful and cheap where I live; in fact, Stockton was once called the Brick City, until they realized the ground settles and shifts so much that the buildings crack. So too will an adobe or cob oven, and they don't hold up in rain without an enclosure. Why not, I thought to myself, just make the bricks myself because I have a kiln? Then they can be any shape and fit together like a puzzle. So what follows are directions for making an oven such as you will find nowhere else. There are no plans per se, just a basic construction principle, which should be pursued in a fit of madness in a single day.

First, dig your clay or buy some low-fire earthenware clay from a supplier. I used 350 pounds of what is called Navaho Wheel 35, seven 50-pound boxes at about $13.50 each, which is about $95. I also bought a nice refractory kiln shelf for $36, the kind that can withstand any amount of heat or abuse without cracking, for the floor of the oven. Two 50-pound bags of sand cost $4.50 each, then 27 cinder blocks for the base at $1.50 each came to about $40. Two 50-pound bags of mortar and a trowel came to $30. Finally an 80-pound bag of stucco mix for the final insulation cost $5. In the end I spent about $215 on materials. You can of course make your oven as big as you like, but it should be at least big enough to hold a nice-size pizza. Keep in mind, the smaller the oven, the easier to fire. There's no sense in heating up a huge oven to bake a few loaves of bread.

Now lay out your cinder blocks. I used a base of eight and then added two additional layers, bringing the whole thing to about waist height. I also added three blocks for a front ledge. No concrete is necessary at this stage. You want the flat side up on the last layer, rather than the side with holes.

Place the kiln shelf on top of the cinder blocks and draw the outline of the shelf with a pencil on the blocks. Next tie the pencil onto a string and tape the end to the center. Inscribe a circle about 4 inches wider than the shelf. This will delineate your clay oven walls. Then draw another circle about 2 inches wider; this will be your stucco insulation layer. It should come to the edge of the cinder blocks. Remove the shelf, and then make a round base of clay 4 inches thick directly on top of the cinder-block base. Score this into squares and carefully number each one. You will be cutting them later, firing them, and then reassembling them in the same order.

Lay a sheet of plastic on top of the clay floor. The bags the clay comes in, cut open, work nicely. It will make getting the sand out later much easier and will prevent the wet sand from mucking up the base. On top of this make a hemispherical mound of wet sand, exactly as you would make a sand castle. Keep in mind that the clay will shrink in firing, and you'll want to have the kiln shelf fit inside later, so mound the sand slightly beyond the original size of the kiln shelf. This will be the size of the oven interior, so make sure it's big enough for a peel, casserole, or whatever you want to cook inside.

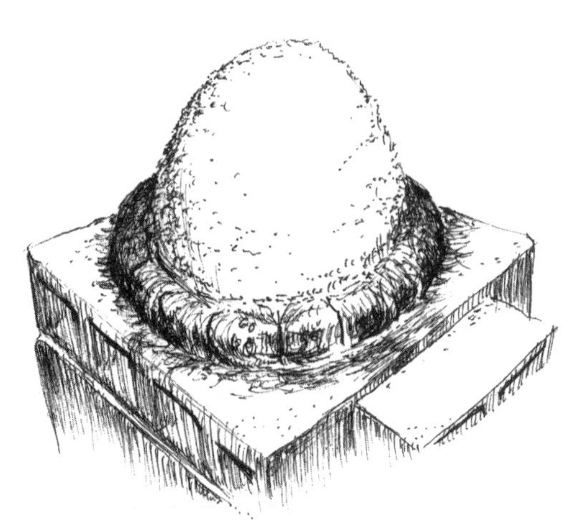

The interior of the oven is formed by heaping a hemispherical mound of wet sand onto which you will pack slabs of wet clay.

Next, cut slabs of clay about 2 inches thick, using a wire tool, and lay them directly on the sand. Fill in the gaps until the whole mound is covered in clay. The trick to making sure the clay adheres is to score it with a pin tool and apply slip—a thick slurry of water and clay. Then repeat the whole process so your walls are 4 inches thick. Remember to score and slip the next layer of slabs, too. Then slap the whole thing all around vigorously into a beautiful dome shape, adding little bits of clay if necessary to make it all even.

Then, with a coil of clay, make a rim where your oven door will go. Remember, you want it wide enough so a peel will slide in. Most important, the oven door must be two-thirds the height of the oven. For some mystical reason this provides the best efficiency. Make two handles for the door. You can make elegant ones by taking a wad of clay in one hand and with the other well moistened, "milk" the clay into a long handle shape. It's a little obscene, but it works. Slice off and affix the handles to the door. Score well the arc of the door, just below the rim. You'll be removing it first.

At the rear of the dome, opposite the door, cut a round hole 3 or 4 inches in diameter, two-thirds from the top, and hand build a chimney with coils of clay. Be fanciful here because this part of the structure will be seen. If you have a wheel you can throw the chimney, too. It can be as high as you like but should be at least a foot or so above the oven roof. Just try not to make it too heavy or it may not stay in place in the end. Cut off the chimney base on an angle, score and add slip, and affix it over the hole you cut. This should be done perhaps a day after you first made the dome, though this depends entirely on the weather. You want it leather hard, as potters say.

Here is the unfired clay oven, the sand having been removed, with a wheel-thrown chimney attached.

Let the whole thing dry some more, so that you can cut it cleanly with a knife. In summer this may be several hours, in a wet cold winter, a few days. Then take string and stretch it around the dome every 4 inches and tug on it just tightly enough so you have lightly scored the clay in straight lines, all around the periphery. When you get to the top you can just eyeball concentric circles. Number these carefully, for the same reason you numbered the base. With a knife (a steak knife over 4 inches long works fine) cut out the chimney with a square section of oven wall. Set it aside gently. Cut out the door; set it aside. The clay must be stiff enough not to bend; if it's not ready, let it dry further. Scoop out all the sand. Then cut out the individual bricks. Each cut should point toward the center of the dome, so that you start horizontally, gradually increasing the angle and then on top you are cutting downward. The angled cut is so that the weight of the dome will be evenly distributed all around and it will hold up once you reassemble it, just like you see in an arch. Then cut each brick vertically, alternating each cut, just like you see on brick houses. The size doesn't matter at all. They don't even have to be very even, as they're all going back together and no one will see them once the insulation is added. Scrape off any remaining sand, but don't worry if there's a little left. Then remove the plastic and cut up the base.

Set all the bricks aside to dry. They must be thoroughly, utterly bone dry. How long this takes is anyone's guess. Test it by kissing a brick; if it still feels cold or wet, wait longer.

Fire the bricks, the door, and the chimney in a kiln, or if you don't have one, ask a potter friend to do it. A single firing to cone 04 or 06 will be perfect, though it will probably take several batches, depending on the size of your oven and kiln. Mine took three firings. Everything will have shrunk a little in firing, but that's fine, it will all go back together.

Mix a bucket of mortar and carefully gob some on each brick, one by one, as you lay them and reassemble the base. Place the kiln shelf on top. Place the ring of the first course of the dome on top, continuing with the mortar and filling the empty space with sand. You'll need the sand just to support your oven while you're reassembling. Add more sand with each completed level until you get to the top. The chimney goes back into place, too. Don't worry if there are a few gaps or if you make a mess with the mortar, like I did. No one will see it.

Next you'll need insulation. Lay on a few inches of stucco made for outdoor use. This is why you made the base larger than the dome; the stucco should now go all the way to the edges, and up the base of the chimney a little, too. You can cover the cinder blocks, too, with plaster or whatever attractive facing you like.

When the stucco is dry, carefully scrape out all the sand and you're ready to fire her up. (You might want to vacuum the oven out; the first pizzas I made had a little sand on them for extra crunch!) Start a fire inside with twigs and small branches. The wood should be absolutely dry. If you have thick logs, they should be split into smaller pieces. Keep adding wood for 1 or 2 hours until the oven is super hot. If you like, get a thermometer; 600° to 700°F is probably about right for baking. But before you put in your dough, you'll need to rake out the ashes and quickly mop the oven floor. The steam is exactly what you need for baking bread. Slide the risen dough into the oven with a long baker's peel. Replace the door and bake, turning the bread around every

This is the finished oven, with insulation in place, being stoked with wood.

so often so one side doesn't burn. Make pizza the same way. You can keep some burning logs going in the rear of the oven. Over time the oven will cool, and that's the time to put in casseroles, roasts, and other foods. The oven should retain heat for many hours or even overnight if you like. At this point you should also name your oven. Mine is Fornax, Roman goddess of ovens and bread.

—K

ACKNOWLEDGMENTS

First thanks go to Monika Verma, our wonderful agent, and Maria Gagliano, our gracious and tireless editor, who was patient enough to invite us back for a second book! We would also like to thank Melissa Broder, our publicist for the first book, whose success meant this second book could exist.

Rosanna's personal thanks go to Ethan Rafal and Della Shea, for the equivalent of bro-hugs and halftime speeches in the locker room of creativity; to Cait Quinlivan, Julia Cattrall, Ally DeArman, and Mitchell McCartney for helping me pull off the domestic stunt of a lifetime; and to Caroline Henderson for going for walks with me while the curds drained.

Enormous thanks go to my parents, who did a remarkable job of passing down their useful skills. In particular, thank you, Papa, for all the help with our wedding rings and for buying the fabric for my first clothing design project. And thanks, Mama, for not only illustrating our second book but for teaching me to braid rugs and letting me loose on your sewing machine at such a young age. I would also like to thank my uncle Hal, who let me help butcher his very last elk.

Ken would like to thank all the wonderful food scholars, family, and friends old and new as well as students who helped inspire, cook, or just consume the fruits of the labor expended in writing this book. I have tried to mention all of you in the recipes themselves, but if I've forgotten anyone, please forgive me.

INDEX

C

D

Q

R

S

T

U

V

W

Y

Z

ABOUT THE AUTHORS

Photo by Norah Hoover

Rosanna Nafziger Henderson grew up on a mountain in West Virginia. She spent her girlhood working in the orchard, planting beans, and selling pies at the farmers' market. Now she translates the traditions of her Appalachian Mennonite upbringing to the urban household on her blog, Paprikahead. A chef, nanny, and editor, she lives with her husband in San Francisco.

Photo by Kann Vaneker

Ken Albala is Professor of History at the University of the Pacific in Stockton, California. He has written numerous books on topics ranging from Renaissance dietetics and courtly dining to beans and pancakes. He has also edited a handful of food reference works and essay collections, several scholarly food series, and coedits the journal *Food, Culture and Society.*